Grand
Conversations
Literature Groups in Action

UPDATED EDITION

Ralph Peterson & Maryann Eeds

New York • Toronto • London • Auckland • Sydney
Mexico City • New Delhi • Hong Kong • Buenos Aires

Our appreciation to the publishers who granted us permission to use excerpts as follows:

From CHARLOTTE'S WEB by E. B. White. Copyright © 1952, and renewed 1980 by E. B. White. Used by permission of HarperCollins Publishers.

From A DAY NO PIGS WOULD DIE by Robert Newton Peck. Copyright © 1972 by Robert Newton Peck. Reprinted by permission of Alfred A. Knopf Inc.

From DOMINIC by William Steig. Copyright © 1972 by William Steig. Reprinted by permission of Farrar, Straus and Giroux, Inc.

From GORKY RISES by William Steig. Copyright © 1980 by William Steig. Reprinted by permission of Farrar, Straus and Giroux, Inc.

From JIM'S DOG MUFFINS by Miriam Cohen. Used by permission of HarperCollins Publishers.

From SYLVESTER AND THE MAGIC PEBBLE by William Steig. Copyright © 1969. Used by permission of the publisher, Simon and Schuster Books for Young Readers, New York.

From TUCK EVERLASTING by Natalie Babbitt. Copyright © 1975 by Natalie Babbitt. Reprinted by permission of Farrar, Straus and Giroux, Inc.

Cover Design: Jorge J. Namerow
Cover Photo: © Guy Call/Stock Connection/Jupiterimages
Interior Design: LDL Designs
Acquiring Editor: Lois Bridges
Production Editor: Sarah Weaver
Copy Editor: Carol Ghiglieri

ISBN-13: 978-0-439-92645-4
ISBN-10: 0-439-92645-9

2 3 4 5 6 7 8 9 10   40   11 10 09

For Leland B. Jacobs,

whose insight, teaching, and spirit

gave life to this book.

Contents

Acknowledgments

We thank Jim Higgins, who gave us our title, and Mary Glover, Linda Sheppard, and Karen Smith—master teachers who responded to our questions about their practice. We also thank Chris Boyd, Roberta Crane, Rhonda Gardner, Mark Routhier, Michelle Wesley, Connie Wigmore, and Beth Zinderman, whose interactions with children we included in the text. Thanks also to the many teachers and students who contributed insights and ideas, especially Carol Christine, Pam Clark, Diana Doyle, Rosalie Lyall, Georgia Peterson, Jean Ross, Kathy O'Neill Shores, Merle Valenzuela, Dwight Vander Schoor, Susan Timmer, Dorothy Watson, Lois Wells, Bev Wilcox, Deidre Nunan and her students, Jeanne Fain, Sarah Hudelson, and Tom Tracy.

Special thanks to Shelley Harwayne for writing the foreword to this edition and to Ardith Cole, Mary Glover, Stephanie Harvey, Lester Laminack, Frank Serafini, Linda Sheppard, and Suzette Youngs for writing tributes to our first edition. Your words have warmed our hearts.

Foreword

I was recently asked to speak at the Guggenheim Museum in Manhattan about the possible relationship between studying art and becoming literate. I began by referring to *Grand Conversations: Literature Groups in Action,* the classic book you hold in your hands. I told the audience of art and literacy educators that the views of the authors, Ralph Peterson and Maryann Eeds, were based on a handful of ideas. Their short list of beliefs reads as follows: "Story is an exploration and illumination of life. Interpretation is the result of a transactional process in which readers bring meaning *to* as well as taking meaning *from* a text. Children are born makers of meaning. Dialogue is the best method for teaching and learning about literature."

I then reread those four statements, substituting words from the artist's world: "Art is an exploration and illumination of life. Interpretation is the result of a transactional process in which museum visitors bring meaning *to* as well as taking meaning *from* a work of art. Children are born makers of meaning, in a library or in a gallery. Dialogue is the best method for teaching and learning about works of art."

The audience couldn't have agreed more, and I wasn't a bit surprised. After all, *Grand Conversations* is a breakthrough book, the one that sent many of us down the glorious path of inviting students to read high-quality literature in our classrooms. I wonder if any other professional book on literacy could pass this "Guggenheim test." What other book treats literature with such integrity and grace that we could apply the teaching and learning principles described to all forms of art?

As a devoted baseball fan, I look forward to the postgame discussions, especially the announcement of the turning point of the game. For me, *Grand Conversations* was the turning point of the game, the book that changed the way we thought about creating literature-based classrooms.

It was the book that so eloquently and simply showed us how to get grand conversations going in our classrooms. We learned to offer only the finest of books to our students, to give them time to read and reread those books, to offer important literary information at the teachable moment, and to demonstrate ever so gently how to engage in meaningful conversations about ideas that really matter. Above all, we learned to trust the books, the children, and ourselves. And we learned to do all of this without any gimmicks, formulas, or motivating devices.

If ever educators needed to read and reread this groundbreaking book, the time is now. The teaching of reading has gotten so complicated, with overwhelmed teachers looking over their shoulders, second-guessing themselves, and wondering if they are following all the rules that have been imposed from above. This book is as much a must-read for beginning teachers as it is for experienced teachers of reading. The former will find just the right dose of information to get started wisely and well. The latter will view this book as a long-needed holiday break, helping to clear the clutter that so easily fills their professional minds and mailboxes.

In their very helpful chapter on literary elements, the authors remind us of the power of metaphor by referring to the arrival of spring in William Steig's *Sylvester and the Magic Pebble*. Spring is a symbol of hope, rebirth, and new beginnings. This reprinting of *Grand Conversations* is the arrival of spring for literacy teachers determined to engage students of all ages in grand conversations about grand books. When teachers pull together to read and respond to Ralph and Maryann's ideas, they will have it in their power to launch a professional journey of hope, rebirth, and new beginnings.

—*Shelley Harwayne*

CHAPTER ONE

Teaching With Real Books

R eal books are wonderful. These are the books you find in public
places like libraries, bookmobiles, bookstores, and sometimes
even supermarkets. Real books rest beside your bed, clutter the coffee
table, and stand on shelves at the ready—waiting to be lifted, opened,
and brought to life by your reading. Real books—each one with its own
individual binding, each one sized just right for the story it houses—are
written by authors who know how to unlock the world with words and
to open our eyes and our hearts. Each real book has its own voice—a
singular, clear voice—and each speaks words that move us toward
increased consciousness.

Teaching with real books is different from teaching with textbooks.
When teachers teach with real books, children choose what they will read,
learn to sample what is available, and find the books appropriate for their
purposes. Textbooks are chosen for the children by others. What will be
read and how it should be responded to is worked out long before the
child receives the book. "Stories" are bound together on standardized
pages for instructional purposes. Each story is linked to activity pages in a
workbook and to additional pages for "enrichment" or "remediation."
Textbooks are more concerned with teaching skills than with presenting
stories so good they simply must be told.

Real books are not outfitted with drills or remedial and enrichment
activities. They do not come imprisoned in boxes and kits, with directions
for usage. Real books have no manuals to tell teachers all the things they
must do and when to do them. The story contained in each book stands
on its own. It is up to teachers and readers to work at interpreting what

the author has written and, once the story is read, to decide what might be done in response. Responses are shared among students, book, and teacher, without the interference of prepackaged thoughts and "answers." Responses are original to those involved and are frequently unpredictable. Teaching is shaped by teachers' beliefs about how children learn best, by their love and knowledge of literature, and by their awareness of children's interests. Life in literature-based classrooms is in a constant state of becoming. Books, children, and teachers all count. There is no prescribed plan to be acted out.

A teacher's view of literature and learning is the greatest determinant of what will happen in a classroom where children read real books. A specific view guides the judgment of what is significant and of value, in both how texts to be read are selected and how the reading of those texts is approached.

Teaching practices guided by textbook programs emphasize mechanical aspects of reading rather than the making of meaning. Stories could just as well be generated by computer (they often sound as though they have been) because the vocabulary is controlled and certain letters and words must be repeated so that they will be "learned."

Those of us who teach with real books acknowledge the importance of the mechanical aspects of learning to read, but we perceive reading as a more complex activity than simply learning to decode letters into sound and finding correct responses to prepared questions. We want children not only to learn how to read, but also to become readers. We consider children's enjoyment and interpretation of literature to be our foremost concern.

Our view of teaching and learning with literature is founded on these four beliefs:

- Story is an exploration and illumination of life.
- Interpretation is the result of a transactional process in which readers bring meaning to as well as take meaning from a text.

TRIBUTE TO THE FIRST EDITION OF
GRAND CONVERSATIONS

A Priceless Guide to Genuine Work With Literature
By Mary Glover

After being a second-grade teacher for many years, I moved up to teach the fourth/fifth-grade class at our school. Although I was an experienced teacher, I'd never taught children older than 7. As I prepared, I decided to use what I knew I could count on—children's literature—as the foundation of all we would do that year. As a "first-year" fourth/fifth teacher, I fumbled my way through math, spelling, and grammar but felt solid and secure with all we did in literature. Years later, I know that my sense of security was grounded in all that I have learned from Ralph Peterson and Maryann Eeds.

Grand Conversations is a synthesis of the work Ralph and Maryann did with many of us years ago at Arizona State University as graduate students, colleagues, and friends. I consider that time to be a pivotal experience in my professional and personal life, and the way Ralph and Maryann approached literature with us then is parallel to what they describe in their book about working with children. They always encouraged us to experience literature for literature's sake, to approach it in a genuine way with our students and on our own. They modeled for us all of the things they asked us to do with children.

Ralph and Maryann set a high standard for approaching literature in classrooms, and they always made me feel like I was smart and had something valuable to offer. As I explored texts in my classroom years later, I remembered to treat my students with that same sense of honoring. Ralph and Maryann helped me pay attention with openness to the ideas of children, and my students never failed to amaze me with their literary insights. I always came away from a literature study changed in some way, in large part due to the grand conversations we had together. *Grand Conversations* is a priceless guide for teachers to find their way back to genuine work with literature, so desperately needed at a time when everything seems to need a number attached to it to be considered of value. I invite you to enter into the dialogue of this extraordinary book written by two even more extraordinary people.

- Children are born makers of meaning.
- Dialogue is the best method for teaching and learning about literature.

In Chapter 3 we will discuss each of these beliefs in more detail, but first we need to outline the components of a literature program, the setting in which it operates, and the human communities that shape it.

CHAPTER TWO

A Literature-Based Reading Program

In our view, a literature-based program that aims toward literacy is made up of four components, each distinct but not separate. The first is story in the home, the beginning of all story and study of story. The other three are school based: sharing story with a group, extensive reading, and intensive reading.

Story in the Home

The study of literature begins with story—the one model for learning that we can be sure children bring with them when they come to school. Children are introduced to story early in their lives and most can tell good stories by the time they are 4 or 5 years old. When we talk of story, we mean the narratives of everyday life, the retelling of something that has happened. Adults, teenagers, and children use the elements of literature naturally in their tellings. They impose a narrative line upon events as a way of bringing order to experiences, as the following examples suggest:

- When they retell what happened, they use a structure which, when discussing literature more formally, we call plot and tension.
- For telling who was there and how they reacted, they use the elements of literature dealing with character and character coping.
- When they reproduce what was said, they give us dialogue.
- When where it all happened is important, they give us place or setting.
- When they talk about how long something lasted or how minutes dragged or accelerated, they give us time—both real and psychological.

- When, as is often the case, the story seems to carry more than just a surface message, they give us symbol and central metaphor.
- How the storyteller conveys these happenings gives us style and language.
- How these events affected the teller determines the mood.

Children also begin to internalize genre as they listen to stories. They know that a story that begins with "When I was a little girl . . ." is different from a story that starts with "Once, long ago in Africa . . ." or "You aren't going to believe what just happened in the parking lot at Safeway . . ." Children are also entirely capable of speaking in metaphor, as in the case of a little boy who held up a bloom of bermuda grass and said, "Look, Mom. A bird flower!" All children come to school with this rich foundation of story. Teachers can expect families to outfit children with a history rich in story before they enter school and throughout their school years.

All homes have stories. While in some families a rich oral exchange of narratives has primacy, in others there is an equal emphasis on reading to children from storybooks, on so-called bedtime reading or lap reading. The home is the starting point, the birthplace of language, and it is to the home that we will return again and again for the support and collaboration on which a literature-based program is built.

Shirley Brice Heath spent years researching the ways different families in different socioeconomic and cultural environments use print and story. In her book *Ways With Words* (1983), she documents how children who have not had certain experiences are set up for failure in a traditional school program. In their book *Growing Up Literate* (1988), Denny Taylor and Catherine Dorsey-Gaines show how many children who are successful must make monumental efforts in the face of more adversity by the time they are 6 than most of us will ever see in a lifetime. In his book *The Meaning Makers* (1986), Gordon Wells shows that for many children the opportunity for quality language interaction drops off markedly in school. All four of these researchers clearly describe the literacy events that permeate the lives of all children—no matter what their backgrounds. They hold up for us to see the diversity and richness of the language all children bring with them. Schools that reject this richness work against literacy. Programs that respect the home and language of children, building on this diverse base, open literacy to all. And it has been our experience that most parents will collaborate with the school when what they have already done with their children is welcomed and valued.

Sharing Stories

We ask you to celebrate the fact that some children entering school have been read to all their lives, know books, have favorite authors and topics and genres, and know what to expect when a story starts "Once upon a time." For those children, a literature-based reading program extends their knowledge. For others who come to school with a tradition of story based more on telling than on reading, a story-reading tradition must be developed.

Both types of children are served through sharing story with the class by reading aloud daily—from all kinds of books, by many different authors, about all kinds of subjects.

ANCHOR THE SOUNDS

The sharing of literature aloud anchors the sounds of the language of literature in the minds of the students. Children of all ages absorb the language they hear. When 5-year-olds hear that William Steig's mean, hungry-looking lion (in *Sylvester and the Magic Pebble*) circled the rock that was Sylvester again and again and finally walked away "confused, perplexed, puzzled and bewildered," there is no need to explain what those words mean. The story and the illustrations provide the meaning and the words are absorbed. Children begin to speak in literature-influenced ways. A little girl said (about herself), "She ran down the hall as fast as her legs could carry her." The assimilation of literary language continues all of one's life, and this assimilation can often be witnessed in children. A fourth-grade group was talking about Katherine Paterson's *The Great Gilly Hopkins*. Their teacher had just read the part in which Gilly reads aloud to Trotter's old blind neighbor the lines from Wordsworth that later lead us to think about the story on another level:

> Not in entire forgetfulness,
> And not in utter nakedness,
> But trailing clouds of glory do we come
> From God, who is our home.

The class was quiet, and then one boy spoke up. "I like those words," he said. "Me, too," echoed others. Articulated meaning will come later, but for now it is enough to anchor the sounds, to give children opportunities to hear "those words."

PROMOTE JOY

Reading aloud is also meant to promote pleasure and enjoyment—to bring joy to life in school. It is no secret that children tend to take up what their parents, teachers, and friends find enjoyable. The enjoyment of a good story, well read, is universal. When teachers share a story by reading it aloud, children are invited to visit imaginary worlds created through words. They are invited to enter into lives, times, and places far removed from daily living. In their imaginations, they can explore the world and the meaning of life by becoming one with characters who search for personal identity, cope with adversity, experience love, and seek acceptance. They are given the opportunity to go after adventure, to struggle for justice, to feel connected to others.

Tribute to the First Edition of
Grand Conversations

Hosting Open Dialogue Among Passionate Readers
By Lester Laminack

Ralph Peterson and Maryann Eeds became my teachers the second I opened my first copy of *Grand Conversations*. When I read the dedication to Leland B. Jacobs, I knew the book would be infused with love of literature and respect for children and teachers.

Ralph and Maryann led me to see the intimate and inextricable connection between building community and hosting open dialogue among passionate readers. I saw the power of focused conversation and the undeniable beauty of children living through a book alongside the characters and becoming part of the fiber of the story. In simple yet eloquent prose, Ralph and Maryann provided guidance, practical advice, forms to help us organize, and suggestions for assessment and evaluation. All this was layered into a deceptively simple package of under one hundred pages.

With its layers of insight that deepen with repeated readings, *Grand Conversations* has been one of those books I revisit time and time again. Each time I return to the text with greater depth and breadth of knowledge, and each time I leave it I am changed by what I have just discovered.

INTRODUCE STUDENTS TO MANY KINDS OF WRITING

Reading aloud gives teachers the opportunity to open up the world of literature to students who may not have discovered it on their own. Amelia Munson, one of the first librarians for young adults, once said that it was her policy to give young people what they wanted to read (even if they were stuck at the level of a Sweet Valley High romance or a Hardy Boys mystery) but also "to set before them what they never knew they wanted." Reading aloud helps students become willing to receive different genres and styles of writing.

BUILD COMMUNITY

Reading aloud also helps a group of diverse students become a community. Communication research tells us that barriers to communication are broken down when individuals live through extraordinary experiences together. We believe that the sharing of literature aloud is one such extraordinary experience. More than once we have noticed members of a group comforting each other when moved to tears by a story read aloud (for example, Robert Coles's *The Story of Ruby Bridges*). More than once we have seen groups develop a collective chill at the end of a creepy Halloween poem (for example, Jack Prelutsky's "The Poltergeist"). More than once we have seen groups laugh aloud at a book and then turn to their neighbors in friendship and warmth (at Barbara Hazen's *Tight Times*, for instance).

Literature knits a group together and contributes to building community. The development of trust and community is necessary to this way of working with literature, for members of the group will be asked to take enormous risks when they are invited to say what they feel and think in front of others. Reading aloud every day accelerates the development of that community more than anything we know.

DEVELOP NEW WAYS OF THINKING ABOUT STORY

Reading aloud also gives children the opportunity to take up ways of thinking about story that can deepen their understanding. Sometimes a comment by the teacher or another student following a selection read aloud can illuminate meaning for all. The time following the reading can be an opportunity for the teacher to "shoot a literary arrow" by commenting on something he or she has noticed about the writing. Children will note similarities with other stories and author styles. And as the year progresses and the number of books read increases, both teacher and students will become outfitted with a rich shared history to draw upon in their collaborative study of literature.

Extensive Reading

The third component of a literature study program is the provision of time for extensive reading on one's own. Children need time to read in peace, to "just read," without worrying about having to do things afterward. Three hundred sixth graders were once asked in a survey how they felt about reading. Had anyone ever done anything to make them dislike doing it? Among the affirmative responses to that question these two ranked the highest: "Made us do book reports" and "Made us answer questions about everything we read."

Providing time for "just reading" means that children actually read during reading time. Learning to read is a continuous, cumulative accomplishment. The skills that make the construction of meaning from a written text possible are never wholly learned. They are continually refined as readers mature by reading. To learn to enjoy making meaning from written text, each person must do the work independently. Children do, as Frank Smith reminds us, learn to read by reading. Teachers and other students can help, but in the end, the individual student must make the effort and do the work. Learners cannot be spectators who watch learning wash over them; they must be participants.

Learning how to construct meaning from different kinds of texts takes practice. Teachers must therefore encourage extensive reading and provide students with extended blocks of time for just reading. Children must be encouraged to read widely and extensively and be challenged to explore new genres and subjects. The goal of the teacher is to expand the students' knowledge of the world through literature. Students are asked to read, as Gary Paulsen says, "like a wolf eats."

Extensive reading is unobtrusive. This is not the time when reflecting on meaning holds sway. Interpretations of what we read will be made, but without conscious deliberation. Though nothing stops us from reflecting on our activity, we take no special note. Our interpretation is guided by the particular interests, background, and experiences we bring to the text. We just read.

We do this kind of reading spontaneously most of our lives. Newspapers, for example, are most often read at this level of consciousness. We stick to a surface level unless the story addresses a topic we know a lot about or offers an opinion we hold or oppose strongly. Normally, no mistrust interrupts the impact of the words.

This is not to say that such reading will not have a direct impact, prompting us to feel and behave differently. It is simply that in extensive reading, text and person blend and we do not take a critical stance. It is lived meaning and not intellectual responding that is valued foremost. We might share what we have read with others, but we do not wrestle with meaning, reading between and behind the lines.

Extensive reading is a time for the reader to become one with the character, to be embedded in the action of the story, to live intensely within the imaginary world created by the author. This is the time readers compile personal literary histories, exploring literary worlds beyond the borders of their lived experience. Students just read!

Intensive Reading

With only the first three components in place—the sense of story children bring with them, the sharing of stories with the group, and the time and resources for extensive reading—you can be sure that children will be provided with golden opportunities to become true readers, people who love literature. But these components also provide the foundation for the fourth component, intensive reading. The next step consists of arranging for the conscious contemplation of a work of literature, the mindful reading that makes up a deeper kind of meaning-making.

Comprehension of a text requires that the reader re-create its meaning, constructing in the light of his or her experience the author's intended meaning. We believe, with Louise Rosenblatt, that reading is a transaction, a bringing meaning to and taking meaning from the written text.

Intensive reading is aimed at giving deliberate thought to the literary experience. Time is spent contemplating meaning—digesting it and giving it what Auden calls "passionate attention."

Good writers always leave gaps for readers to fill in. Wolfgang Iser, in his book *The Act of Reading* (1974), calls these "blanks" and points out that, as a reader's mind works to fill in these blanks, an "act of constitution" takes place (p. 167). We bring our lived experiences and our literary histories to our reading. The author gives us words and blanks—and as we read the lines and between the lines, the text is brought to life. When children read that Max "sailed back over a year and in and out of weeks and through a day and into the night of his very own room where he found his supper waiting for him and it was still hot," they suddenly have another view of how Max got to the land of the wild things. A gap is filled. When children go from 11-year-old Winnie Foster's adventure in saving Ma Tuck to Pa Tuck's reading of Winnie's gravestone, they must leap to the understanding that she never drank the water but grew old and eventually died—someone's beloved wife and mother.

This kind of interpretation is critical in nature and does not run along quietly in the background of our perceptions the way meaning does in extensive reading. In intensive reading, we give conscious attention to what is written and not written. We make deliberate inquiries into what the story is about. We examine and weigh possible interpretations.

There is no doubt that some children and adults are more adept than others when it comes to illuminating meaning by seeing into the words shaped by authors. Each reader interprets the text in the light of his or her lived or imaginary life, culture, background, hopes, fears, and, at times, guilt. Just as each story has its own voice, each reader hears that voice in his or her own way. Through critical interpretation, children and teachers expand a text's potential for meaning by sharing their insights and the connections they have made. A story need not be one story in itself but can be many stories, corresponding to the many attitudes and backgrounds of the individual readers.

TRIBUTE TO THE FIRST EDITION OF
GRAND CONVERSATIONS

Creating a "Conversation Curriculum" for the Classroom
By Ardith Davis Cole

Those of us who have been involved in the literature circle knee-to-knee process for the last decade remain ever grateful to Ralph Peterson and Maryann Eeds, for it was they who inspired us into the "grand conversation" model. In the late 1980s, Ralph and Maryann restructured my thinking when they discussed dialogue as pedagogy. This substantive theory, later described in their *Grand Conversations* book, offered all of us an exciting new doorway into literacy. We wanted our children to experience literature-based programs that create community, promote joy, prompt extensive and intensive reading, view children as meaning-makers, and allow text interpretation to be a shared experience. It was, therefore, with their theory in hand that I began developing a conversation curriculum in my own classroom.

Grand Conversations changed our teaching-learning perspective and helped us see all children as knowledgeable, passionate learners whose voices can drive the literacy process in exciting new ways. This new edition offers all of us a special gift from two professionals who have spent a lifetime investigating grand conversations.

The process of possessing a work can be aided by sharing interpretations with other readers who are enjoying the same text. Therefore, intensive reading is most often practiced in small literature study groups. These groups typically have up to eight members, and each member shares his or her thoughts and feelings about the book with other readers.

In practice, teacher and students might begin by sharing impressions, ideas, and problems they encountered in constructing meaning. When a topic surfaces that commands the group's interest and has a potential for altering perception, the talk shifts from sharing to dialogue. Through dialogue, the group (teacher and students together) works to disclose meaning, thereby potentially expanding the meaning of the work for all participants. Because a text's meaning is embedded in the mood of the story, in the ordering of time, in the creation of place, in the way the characters cope and develop, in the story structure, in the point of view, and in the use of language and symbols, these elements of literature will surface naturally through dialogue. Working collaboratively, the group spends time contemplating meaning and digesting it. Group members help each other begin to *see* where previously they may have only *looked*. Our job as teachers is to help with this seeing.

We use the word *dialogue* rather than *discussion* to describe that very specific set of group interactions in response to good books, and we have (we think) good reasons for doing so. The word *discussion* does not convey the intensity and involvement that must be present in intensive reading.

More than an exchange of information and sharing of ideas, dialogue requires personal investment. It cannot be pursued passively. Teachers who choose dialogue see it as a dynamic process. Dialogue is demanding work, requiring that all involved have initiative and wide-awake imaginations. Tension and anxiety are not foreign to it. In fact, dialogue ceases when participants exempt themselves from the necessity of exerting intelligence and imagination.

Meaning evolves in dialogue through heartfelt responding that seeks to cooperatively disclose meaning. People in dialogue need each other. They collaborate with one another, striving to comprehend ideas, problems, events, feelings. Working together, partners in dialogue call one another forth as they seek to comprehend the world.

Summary

Collaboration with the home, sharing of story with the group, provision for extensive reading, and gathering together in groups for intensive, contemplative reading are interdependent. What occurs in one area will influence the others. Each is a powerful component of a reading/literature program.

CHAPTER THREE
Beliefs and Practices

What are some of the specifics teachers employ when they work with literature? And how do these teachers convey to their colleagues how they do what they do?

When we first began writing this chapter, we thought we would spell out useful strategies or tactics for teachers to use. We planned to reflect on how we and others teach literature, and describe the process in operational terms. But the results read like a recipe and failed to capture what we really experience when we are teaching. So often strategies are plans originated outside a living encounter, then passed along from one teacher to another, and collected in "how-to" books for use in any situation. We wanted instead to convey how we go about responding to the leads that children always give us as we work with them and with literature.

In the end we realized that in spelling out what we do, we would fail to reveal the essence of it. It's an old problem for teachers: what is truly significant cannot be put down in so many words. We don't work out in advance what is going to happen when we teach. Instead, we prepare ourselves carefully to respond to what might happen within a living encounter. We rely on timing and our ability to seize the moment, always realizing that if one moment passes unrecognized, another is on its way. Responses flow out of what we believe and know. With that in mind, we decided that a section dealing with what we do when we work with literature should first spell out the four beliefs we hold, and then use examples to illustrate how these beliefs translate into concrete actions.

Story Is an Exploration and Illumination of Life

Writers make stories for people to live in as carpenters make houses. While living within the story world, readers have access to insights, experiences, and perceptions they would otherwise not have available. A story illuminates what it is to be human as it describes the joys, triumphs, and sorrows of specific characters. By being aesthetically ordered, the literary form makes accessible the most fundamental experiences of life: love, aloneness, belonging, alienation, hopelessness, hope. Feeling becomes thinkable through the story form.

All it takes for readers to have access to a particular "story world which is but never was" is a willingness to enter. Our imagination is a keyhole through which we witness the most private events of people's lives, experience someone else's fate as our own, and are transported to times and places never accessible to us otherwise. The possibilities of human life are illuminated, both the good and the evil, and we are free to explore, to take sides, to experience, to learn, but without the dire consequences we sometimes encounter in our physical world. When we read a story, we truly merge heart and intellect.

Interpretation Is a Transactional Process

We chose the word *interpretation* over the word *comprehension* very thoughtfully. Comprehension emphasizes the text. Questions asked in the teacher's manuals and on tests are assumed to have "right" answers, but these fail to account for the individual's lived and literary histories. Readers are asked to read for standardized responses and not think for themselves. They are not asked to think in original ways that reflect their experiences, thereby making meaning on their own. In textbook teaching, someone else does the thinking; teachers and children are actors in someone else's puppet play.

We believe that genuine meaning, meaning over which readers have ownership, arises only if those readers are able to structure it themselves, through their own interpretations, in the light of their experiences and their intent. It is in this way that the text is brought to life. We make story appear as an image. We form feelings of joy, despair, happiness, and fear by interacting with the text. We experience the fate of the characters as our own because of our willingness to interpret—to breathe life into—the text. We make something that is not yet there come to life by giving meaning to the words.

For all reading, including story reading, the interpretive act is transactional. Readers simultaneously bring meaning to and take meaning from the text as they read. In the making of meaning, readers are both passive and active participants. Interpretation is so natural to us that we pay no attention to it, as we don't to many other ordinary things in life. Our interpretations vary with our experiences, our attitudes, our personal literary histories, and our purposes. When interpretations are shared with a community of readers, different people's interpretations enhance the potential for making meaning for all.

We view readers of any age as individuals who project meaning in the process of making meaning. Story calls upon readers to give themselves to an imaginary world and to make that world live by bringing to it unique interpretations resulting from their life experiences, their reading histories, and their life's hopes.

We believe that children learn to make meaning from texts by practicing this action alongside makers of meaning who are more experienced than they are. Children benefit from demonstrations by teachers and classmates who show the way. Practice accompanied by feedback is essential. But because the expressive character of meaning construction—the projecting of meaning—remains mostly hidden, educators have slipped into treating meaning-making as a passive action that can be controlled by instructional materials.

Six-year-old Casey was looking at the picture of Sylvester as a rock in winter in William Steig's *Sylvester and the Magic Pebble*. The picture shows a blizzard, with snow covering everything—including the rock that is Sylvester. The text reads:

Then it was winter. The winds blew, this way and that. It snowed. Mostly, the animals stayed indoors, living on the food they had stored up.

One day a wolf sat on the rock that was Sylvester and howled and howled because he was hungry.

Casey says, "It's a good thing he's a rock!" The teacher looks confused—Casey is supposed to understand that it is not a good thing to have turned oneself into a rock. "Why do you say that, Casey?" she asks, genuinely curious at his unexpected comment. "Because," says Casey, as though it were obvious, "otherwise he would have been eaten up! Because it says the wolf was hungry!"

Here Casey makes a unique interpretation that had not occurred to the teacher. She is enriched by his insight, he by the respect she shows for his idea.

In another conversation about the same book, Tracy (enumerating the things she thought were funny about the book) says, "When Sylvester finds the red pebble—and the ducks are cute . . ."

TEACHER: The what?

TRACY: The ducks are cute. [*She points to a picture of ducks looking around in amazement because first it was raining, then the rain suddenly stopped, then started again.*]

TEACHER: The ducks are cute. They've got their bills up in the air like they're just enjoying the sunshine, having a grand time, uh-huh.

TRACY: Or else they're thinking, "How'd that happen?"

TEACHER: How'd what happen?

TRACY: The rain started, then stopped.

TEACHER: Yes! Of course they're thinking that!

TRACY: They go, "It started a little while ago—what happened?"

TEACHER: You know what I was doing? All I was doing was looking at the picture.

In this dialogue, the teacher is dumbfounded by the discovery that she, but not 6-year-old Tracy, had missed a subtle point of interpretation. You can expect this to happen often when children become collaborators in building meaning rather than receivers of someone else's transaction with the text. Events depicted in a book may be interpreted differently by children and teachers.

Different interpretations of total works also occur. In fact, ideas of what constitutes an author's "message" to a reader almost always differ for individual readers. Interpretations of Nikki Giovanni's poem "Ten Years Old," for example, can vary dramatically with the composition of the group reading it. In this poem, a small boy gets himself cleaned up, gets a new haircut, rides on the bus by himself to a large city library, walks past the lions and the guard up to the desk, and asks to see the "Dr. doo little steroscope please." But the librarian asks him if he has a library card. He replies that he lives up the street, but she only repeats the question "Do You Have a LIBRARY Card?" Another lady intervenes and says to the librarian: "GIVE THE BOY WHAT HE WANT. HE WANT TO LEAD THE RACE."

Some readers of this poem (adults in this case) insist that the little boy has gone to the library determined to be the first one in a race with other members from his classroom (who visited the library in the spring) to view Dr. Doolittle on the stereoscope. Others take a different view of the words of the second woman and speculate that she may have been interpreting the boy's new haircut, his shiny knees, his unwillingness to back down, his presence in a library during summer vacation, as leading another race—for knowledge? For experience? Others insist he is a budding Martin Luther King Jr. and represents his race. But no matter what an individual's original interpretation of the poem is, it is rare to find anyone who doesn't feel that his or her understanding is enhanced by the sharing of the diverse interpretations of the group.

Tribute to the First Edition of
Grand Conversations

The Power of Honoring Students' Experiences
By Suzette Youngs

Grand Conversations continually reminds me to have faith in children's eagerness to become critical readers and thinkers. When I listen to students' interpretations of the wonderful literature we read, my own understanding is richer. The book has supported me over the years as an intermediate classroom teacher, and each time I come back to it, my understanding has changed because I have a new lens from which to read. Children leave my classroom believing in themselves as readers as a result of our conversations. Even when they find themselves in places where literature discussions aren't supported, they create their own discussion groups. Clearly, students understand what Ralph and Maryann meant when they wrote, "story is an exploration and illumination of life" and "children are born makers of meaning."

It is helpful to think of the process of interpretation or meaning-making as taking two forms. "Just reading" is an unconsidered, unexamined response—a first step in reading story. The second form takes place when readers deliberate over the meaning of a text and consciously shape the meaning they make. At these times teachers and children take pleasure in inquiring into the text and consciously make connections.

Growth takes time. Establishing the value of literature and nurturing a critical disposition is more of a quest than an objective; therefore, the notion of approximation is important. As teachers, we are concerned that our students' interpretations are evolving, that growth is occurring, rather than whether or not a particular prepackaged interpretation is being conveyed.

Children Are Makers of Meaning

Some time ago Frank Smith shared the observation that you learn to read by reading. It was a surprising and challenging notion then, but it seems so obvious now. "Of course," we think, "that is how you learn to read—you *read.*" It seems too simple, too ordinary. Could it be that the elaborate technologies, the carefully designed systems developed over so many decades to teach children to read are unnecessary? Could it be that children learn to read by reading in the presence of people interested in helping them make meaning from texts? Could it be that learning to read is like learning to speak?

We believe so. When children live in an environment where real text is in constant meaningful use, and where they are writing and creating their own texts, they will learn to construct meaning from print, just as children actively involved in home life learn to speak.

Teachers using literature teach by example and help children perceive themselves as creators of meaning. Children will come to see themselves as readers who bring their own meaning to the text in an authoritative way, who share their interpretations with others, and who listen to what others have to say. They become critics of literature, and they grow both in their expectations of literature and in their aesthetic experience.

In literature-based programs, students are helped to become collaborators. By supporting tolerance of the opinions and interpretations of others, by recognizing that interpretations will vary, and by learning to cope with ambiguity, teachers help children stretch the boundaries of their own knowing. Children learn to enjoy the activity of making meaning and become able participants in the give and take of its construction. They learn first to take delight in the meaning others disclose, and then learn to revise their own thinking when there are reasons to do so.

Getting children to see themselves as makers of meaning is not a simple and easy matter. The attitudes and skills involved are not there merely for the taking; they must be learned.

First, children must be helped to recognize their part in creating meaning. A child (or an adult) might be good at engaging in dialogue about pets, games, or family and still have no ear for what might be said in response to a story. It is at times a struggle to draw children beyond "I liked" and "I didn't like" responses. Perceptive and informed responses are possible, even from the very young, but they are not likely to happen on their own. Children need teachers to demonstrate how to enter into and explore the world of literature, just as children learning language need adults who show them how language functions in the everyday world.

Silence is likely to be the first problem teachers encounter when they share literature with students. Experienced teachers, early in the school year, anticipate that their call of "What do you think?" may be greeted by closed lips. Once students understand that the teacher is truly interested in what they have in mind, most will begin to project their meaning into the discussion. But for some it will be a long struggle. Some children are not aware of the power they have to create meaning with literature. Teachers can only be patient, keep working, demonstrate without dominating, and trust that this awareness will come with continued opportunity.

There are also children in most classrooms who restrict their participation to listening. They are ready to take in what others have to offer and tell it back if asked, but they are not willing to thrust their own ideas and experiences into the encounter. Perhaps their previous experiences have made them believe that truth comes only from others, and they are now programmed to store other people's knowledge and feed it back.

Helping these children perceive themselves as having worthwhile experiences and ideas to contribute is a teaching challenge. Reluctant students are not always visible in traditional textbook programs. The materials in a basal system are designed for silence and for predictable responses, and children are not asked to assume responsibility for the creation of meaning. They and the teacher act out someone else's plan, complete someone else's thinking. But in a literature-based program, reluctant students quickly become visible. A program built on viewing children as active participants in making meaning is one in which teachers are constantly monitoring the participation of all students. They will always need to be ready to respond to situations of the moment, including nonresponses. Sustained silence on the part of some students requires a teacher's utmost skills, for at no time must a child be bullied into responding or made to look inferior by constant and inappropriate prodding on the part of the teacher.

Collaboration Is Essential

Collaboration is our favored way of working. The spirit of collaboration is essential in constructing meaning. Teachers work together with children, and children with children, to initiate responses, share interpretations, and construct meaning. This messy process involves a certain amount of groping, questioning, and putting forth of promising beginnings in the hope that others will contribute to the completion. This way of working encompasses both inquiry and critique, as the base for comprehending a text is broadened. Children practice making meaning as they make personal connections to the text and benefit from the insights of others.

Teachers work alongside their students, negotiate meaning with them, and take into account their perspectives—what they know or don't know. Information is supplied to fill specific needs, and meaning is simplified to sustain inquiry. Certainly this is the most difficult and challenging kind of teaching. Teachers must be listeners who avoid domination and act collaboratively. They must trust that by collaborating, students will not only learn about literature but also practice a process of acting and reflecting—making inquiries and critiquing—that will help them learn how to learn.

Dialogue Is the Best Pedagogy

We believe that the dialogue model is the best system for students to use in text interpretation. Why dialogue? Because it is a natural way for people to learn and to construct meaning. The lecture model places knowledge outside the students, treating them as passive recipients; dialogue recognizes that knowledge is something students actively construct. Listening to lectures is a solitary activity. Dialogue is a process of coproducing meaning. Dialogue partners need one another's patience, ideas, and encouragement. The give-and-take nature of the system depends on other participants to take up an idea, expand it, and add to it.

Participants in dialogue experience in a dramatic way what it means to construct meaning. For the most part, our individually constructed meaning happens unnoticed. But in a group we can take note of the shifts in thinking that occur as the interpretation of the text evolves. Group members also learn about the feelings and experiences of others as they interact. Members seek to know ideas on other people's terms as they collaborate in the construction of meaning.

Dialogue encompasses inquiry and critique—skills necessary for constructing meaning. Some people question whether children are knowledgeable enough to engage in critique. They feel that knowledge of facts must come before the ability to judge. While it is true that a critique is of little value if the critic has not lived perceptively with the facts, it does not necessarily follow that children are incapable of critique.

Human beings seem to have a nascent ability to judge. Current language-acquisition research makes it clear that it is through testing (judging) the effectiveness of language strategies that young children gain control over language. It is our experience that exercising critique in a collaborative form (such as dialogue) is an excellent way to help children grow in their ability to construct meaning. Dialogue provides the following:

- Practice in learning to attend to the facts
- Practice in discriminating among values, within a context that naturally provides demonstrations
- Relevant feedback

Dialogue has its tough moments, when ambiguity prevails and tension mounts. After all, meaning is being examined from different perspectives. This can be, and usually is, a messy process. The spirit of collaboration is tested. When the going gets tough, teachers need to remember that teaching is easy only when students are asked to become simple consumers of conventional views. Teachers who use dialogue as a means for interpreting a text must value the dynamic, ever-changing character of meaning-making that results when children are called upon to see for themselves. The words "I think I'm changing my mind" should come to be valued, whether uttered by students or teachers.

Two simple rules help promote effective dialogue. The first is to respect the interpretations of others and help in their development whenever possible. It is not necessary to adopt these varying interpretations, but everyone is obliged to listen to them and give them full consideration. The second rule is that participants—teachers and students—must not enter dialogue with an agenda in mind. Spontaneity is essential. It is the immediacy of the responding, and the listening, that moves participants to insights that cannot be realized through solitary thinking. Teachers, of course, know the story under discussion and have prepared for the dialogue by exploring the possibilities for interpretation. They have some ideas about direction and purpose. But they nevertheless maintain a healthy uncertainty, an ability to live in the moment, which leaves them open to respond to whatever emerges within the encounter. An inevitable course is not charted in advance. Such teaching requires risk taking for both teachers and children.

Dialogue is at the same time difficult and enjoyable. It is difficult because it requires initiative, inquiry, critical thinking, and invention from all involved. In fact, dialogue ceases when participants exempt themselves from exerting intelligence and imagination. It is enjoyable not only because teachers have a chance to see ideas come to life and then be developed by collaborators in a dynamic way, but also because the possibility exists that an original way of viewing, a fresh perspective, will evolve. By engaging children in inquiry and reflective thought, the process of dialogue helps children learn to express their ideas effectively and to make increasingly accurate representations of reality.

Dialogue really comes to life when children draw on their own experiences and base their responses on their own lives, by means of either a rationally formed knowing or hunches based on their feelings. Human beings cannot be expected to engage in dialogue about something they're neither informed about nor interested in.

The following facets of dialogue, which either originate from or are consistent with the findings of language-acquisition research, are useful to keep in mind.

APPROXIMATION

Accepting approximations is fundamental. Just as parents accept children's first attempts to talk, expecting that they will eventually be able to communicate more precisely, so teachers must accept that children will grow in their understanding and appreciation of literature. Competence is achieved over time, and we concern ourselves with the direction of the responses children make to literature every bit as much as the specific content of those responses. Children are encouraged and coaxed to share their thinking. Responses are not judged in terms of right or wrong, but they are looked at in terms of direction. Will the path being followed lead to improved interpretations?

DEMONSTRATION

Now that communication is dominated by television and the Internet, teachers frequently have to win children over to the beauty and power of literature, to demonstrate the joys and rewards that exist in the world of story. Teachers need to show what story means to them in their own lives—how the story lives in them. With their own laughter and tears, they demonstrate the power words can have to bring joy and laughter, sorrow and remorse. They demonstrate the value of books by their actions, and share with children the insights that literature brings them. Teachers are the leading critics in the classroom; they point the way to searching out the potential of a text. By thinking openly and making their judgments visible to children, teachers demonstrate a way for children to find their own voices and take their own initiatives in constructing meaning.

PRACTICE AND FEEDBACK

Practice and feedback go hand in hand. Children need numerous opportunities to practice entering authors' story worlds and sharing their interpretations with others. It takes time and practice to develop the attitudes, knowledge, and habits required for recreating meaning from texts and sharing our insights with others. It takes time and practice to develop the ability to be attentive to the ideas of others and to respond to those ideas. It takes the discriminating feedback of teachers and fellow students to make individuals aware of their successes.

SIMPLICITY

Finally, we believe that it is best to keep the teaching plan simple.

The books will offer the story necessary for dialogue. Real books, grand books, will produce grand conversations.

Teachers must come to trust themselves to grow in their own ability to read and talk about a book with insight and clarity—to become aware of the times when the work in a literature study group goes beyond mere sharing to an opportunity for true dialogue. Accept approximation in yourself as you accept it in your students. Good teaching takes time. We must be patient with ourselves as well as with our students as we make our way. We are all learners.

CHAPTER FOUR
Literary Elements

In the next chapter we want to describe how some of our colleague teachers have organized their literature groups. But before we do, we want to discuss literary elements: character, time, mood, and so on. If your own experiences are like ours, at various secondary and post-secondary levels you had to master these terms, but in a way that made them seem an end in themselves. We may have been told how an aware-ness of them could deepen our experiences with particular works of liter-ature, but we don't remember much practice with them, nor many oppor-tunities for us to have a say.

But we have learned since, and continue to learn, that a gradual increase in awareness of how various authors use these elements in partic-ular stories enables us to enter ever further into story worlds and see and understand them much better. It is the interaction of the elements of lit-erature that brings story into existence.

We believe that awareness of literary elements and of their function in a story nurtures the development of children's ability to respond imagina-tively to a text. More than that, through the study of literature, children will grow in their appreciation of the craft of writing, and their own writ-ing will benefit. We pay attention to story elements in the specific study of literature, but they also help organize what is talked about in our writing conferences, as children gain insight, for instance, into developing place, ordering time, and changing the point of view of a story. Studying and writing stories of their own helps children gain insight into how writers work to create story, and how they might improve their own craft. All teachers of literature take delight in finding the fruit of their teaching on the pages of a child's story. Teachers seeking to improve their students' writing have no choice but to turn to the study of literature. In the final analysis, it is authors who teach our children to write.

Teachers differ over whether to instruct children in the elements of literature or not. As we have said, it is possible to construct meaning from a text without being specifically conscious of these elements. But our own experiences have shaped our view that it is difficult to teach about story without making the elements visible. And we have found that even the youngest are capable of understanding and responding to them.

Linda Sheppard examined three of Maurice Sendak's stories with her kindergarten class: *In the Night Kitchen, Outside Over There,* and *Where the Wild Things Are.* Together they decided that each of the three books was circular, portrayed powerful children who made trips to unusual places, showed bravery, contained three magic moves, and was scary. In coming to these conclusions, the children talked about story structure, characters, and mood. No formal instruction was necessary. The functions of the various elements simply unfolded within the dialogue around these well-loved stories.

The question is not so much whether children will learn about literary elements, but how. We oppose decontextualized direct teaching of them and favor naming them in the context of sharing story, when the time is right. Story elements provide insight into levels of story meaning that may otherwise go unremarked. Talking about them provides us with a pathway for entering the text in the study of literature.

Layers of Story Meaning

Teachers of literature want children to be more than plot readers. They want them to get beyond book-jacket reporting to interpreting story at different levels of meaning. Plot readers will know who lived, who died, and who broke a leg, but they will not reap the true rewards of attending carefully to what is evolving at various levels in the story. For literature

TRIBUTE TO THE FIRST EDITION OF
GRAND CONVERSATIONS

"Shooting Literary Arrows" Into Discussions of Literature
By Frank Serafini

I was first introduced to the material to be contained in *Grand Conversations* during my graduate studies with Ralph and Maryann at Arizona State University. Every time I revisit the book, I hear Ralph talking about the importance of dialogue and Maryann discussing the need for teachers to respect a piece of literature and find ways to gently "shoot literary arrows" into our literature study discussions.

Since my time as a graduate student, my own research and writing about literature-based reading programs have been heavily influenced by the concepts and practices described in *Grand Conversations*. This deceptively simple book is one that I revisit each and every summer as I gear up for the children's literature classes I teach at the university.

Two things resonate each time I reread this book. First, the amount of faith Ralph and Maryann have in literature to illuminate life, and second, the tremendous faith they have in children not to miss what is being offered. Ralph and Maryann teach us not to simply use literature to teach reading, but to experience literature in order to understand ourselves and the world more completely.

In *Grand Conversations*, Ralph and Maryann share their love of literature, their respect for story, and some instructional strategies to help students develop a greater appreciation of the structures and elements that authors draw upon to weave their stories. The book is a must-read for every classroom teacher and university professor who spends time with children and literature.

studies, we restrict our choices to books that have layers of story action and meaning. Multilayered books contribute more dramatically to the feelings readers experience and the thoughts they create, and make the resolution of the central story conflict more compelling. It is possible to read Patricia MacLachlan's *Sarah, Plain and Tall* without attending to how the story is moved along by the simplicity of the prairie setting, without being aware of the part music plays in symbolizing the loss felt by Caleb and Anna, or without being aware of the importance of color in building our anticipation as well as bringing unity to the text, but much of the richness of the book will be lost if these levels are not explored.

Imagine reading Natalie Babbitt's *Tuck Everlasting* and not being conscious of how weather is used to help create and resolve tensions, or reading *Sylvester and the Magic Pebble* and missing how William Steig uses the seasons to guide our feelings of hopelessness and hope. Much of the story is lost in *Tuck Everlasting* if we fail to take note of early signals that Winnie will change from being the passive child of an overbearing mother and grandmother to someone who takes charge and is in every sense her own person. Story moves at different levels. The more your students become aware of these levels, the more they will perceive the complexity of the story structure, and the richer their interpretative competence will be.

In discussing Meindent Dejong's *The House of Sixty Fathers*, one fifth-grade dialogue group was particularly moved by how Tien Pao responded as each frightful event of the story unfolded. One child after another cited events they found particularly meaningful. One child noted that every event had something to do with family: the loss of it when Tien Pao is so frighteningly separated; the substitution for it when Tien Pao is found by a wounded airman and they help each other; the symbolic representation of its loss when Tien Pao's little group of ducks is swept away in their dishpan while one who has fallen out desperately paddles to catch up; the substitute fathers in the persons of airmen who adopt him as their project; and the final impossible but satisfying reunion, when he picks his own mother's face out of thousands. Suddenly the group saw how these incidents contributed to the story meaning they had experienced. They came to a greater appreciation of Dejong's genius in singing this song to the power of love, which can bind together as a family such diverse people as a lost Chinese 6-year-old and a 36-year-old wounded American pilot.

Through the exploration of how the characters coped within the story events, a possible central metaphor for the book—the idea of the family—was discovered, enriching the understanding of all the participants.

Readers do not give their imaginations a workout when they attend exclusively to the plotline of a story, and the rewards of reading are therefore sparse. The complication that results from tracking story movement at various levels makes imaginative interpretation possible. But we must proceed with caution and not push our students. Changes in perception take time. We nurture awareness of the levels of story movement when the time seems right.

But we also prepare ourselves carefully for the right time. On our second read through the book, we note points where the children are likely to raise ideas that might lead to dialogue about levels of story meaning. We often use sticky notes to mark places we believe will be significant. Other teachers underline, or write in the back, or keep a separate pad of preparation notes. When we ask children to do the same thing, they often mark spots that become starting points for talking about levels of story meaning.

Structure

Kay Vandergrift, in her book *Child and Story* (1980), points out that the structure of story is more than just beginning, middle, and end. The overall design gives unity and coherence to all the elements of story. Structure encompasses story incidents that bring about movement at various levels, thereby creating and resolving dramatic tensions. In thinking about structure, it is helpful to be aware of plot and tension.

PLOT

Plot, the narrative sequence, is surely the most overworked element of literature in a textbook reading program. It is the most accessible, and consensus about what makes up plot is usually easily reached. Plot sticks to the surface level and requires a minimum of interpretation on the part of the reader. Many book reports never get beyond outlining the plot and only demonstrate to the teacher that a book has been read.

Plot is important, of course, as the meaning we make in reading is dependent, at the very minimum, upon responding to the narrative sequence, by interpreting how incidents are related—how one event adds to or leads to another. It is through the ordering of incidents that the author evokes the feelings we experience as readers.

TENSION

Exaggerated attention to plot focuses too much on what happens in the story and not enough on what the reader experiences. We know the plot of a story only after the fact, for only when the reading is completed can we decide what the plot was. The notion of tension, on the other hand, is always present in our reading, pulling us along, challenging us to stretch our imaginations. In emotional terms, tension might be referred to as the suspense, anxiety, nervousness, strain, urgency, excitement, or fear that grips us as we read.

Two characteristics stand out. First, all tensions are not of equal interpretive value. For instance, while the tension that arises from a character coping within a specific incident might contribute to interpreting the main line of the story, it need not necessarily be a major tension in the story itself.

In William Steig's *Caleb and Kate* there are several important incidents that make us feel anxious and hold us in suspense: Caleb being unable to speak more than a suffering growl; Kate searching for Caleb, worried that a catastrophe has befallen him; Caleb discovering the seductive joy of being a dog among dogs; the prevailing sense of hopelessness as each attempt Caleb makes to gain his true identity fails. All these incidents can be said to contribute to the central story line, and they build meaning and suspense together, but in themselves they do not have the breadth of concept to be a major or central tension. A central tension would be whether Caleb will ever return to his rightful shape (he has been turned into a little red dog by the wicked witch Yedida) and be reunited with his wife, who believes she has driven him away with her cantankerous behavior.

The major tension in a story integrates a wide range of story action. We draw out opinions by simply asking the children what they think the story is about. Patience is necessary. Constructing meaning takes practice and feedback from an experienced reader. It may take a couple of days for reflection to produce a new understanding of the meaning of the story.

During the first read of a story, we read with what might be called a working hypothesis. When we later revisit the book, we often find that the whole has come together in a new light. There need not be a single interpretation of what a story is about (which is not to say that all are of equal value), and in working with students it is a good idea to explore several possibilities. Our focus should be on developing the students' abilities to construct meaning consciously.

The notion that tensions shift as we read is important as well. At any time during our experience with a text, the meaning we project is in keeping with what we consider the story to be about at that moment. The hypothesis we are working with at any one time pulls us to see relationships, to connect incidents, to view events in light of one another, and to anticipate future events—in short, to make meaning. But as we read, we usually also make adjustments in what we think the story is about. If the meaning we are constructing ceases to make sense, we back up, shift our perspective, and start again.

This is where children and teachers help one another. Dialogue puts forward a new story line, puts events and relationships into a new light. Our basis for interpreting the text is broadened. In working together to disclose a deeper level of meaning, each participant's imagination is enriched and the potential for meaning construction is expanded. This is one reason why adults read the work of professional critics, whose business it is to pay attention to the details and bring forth original interpretations by disclosing meaning that lies hidden.

For example, the central tension that first appears to move Caleb and Kate along might be whether Caleb will ever become himself again, or whether he will be destined to live out his life as a dog while his wife is forced to suffer the mystery of his disappearance. Later, thinking sparked by dialogue might propose that the central tension could be whether or not Caleb and Kate's relationship will be reestablished, and possibly enriched, due to the mischance that befell them.

Multilayered stories artfully maintain tension and keep the reader going through phases of uncertainty and questioning. Tension builds to a final resolution that leaves the reader with a satisfying feeling that loose ends are tied.

For this reason, we find that stories that are episodic in nature, with a slight tension building to a resolution in each chapter, do not lend themselves as well to literature study. In contrast, with a book like *Sarah, Plain and Tall,* readers experience a shift in the tension central to the story. We first become involved when 6-year-old Caleb asks to be told again a familiar story about his birth, causing us to question what happened to his mother. When later he asks his papa why he doesn't sing anymore, the father replies that he has forgotten the old songs but perhaps has found a way to get them back, and we, as readers, experience a feeling of loss again. The father then reveals that he has placed an advertisement for a wife and has received a reply, and Caleb says to "ask her if she sings." Another layer of tension then builds as Sarah comes to visit and both father and children wonder if she will choose to leave her beloved Maine coast to stay on the desolate prairie with them.

Incidents are essential to the narrative structure of story. But incidents are also instruments for making us experience tension. Thus they contribute to, and to some degree guide, interpretation. They are the vehicle through which readers experience the complications confronting characters as they cope to resolve conflicts.

It is helpful for teachers and children to focus their attention in specific ways so that aspects of plot and tension will be revealed. Children can try to identify the tensions that pull them along in their reading of the story. In *Sarah, Plain and Tall*, for example, very simple incidents (like collecting wildflowers to dry or leaving hair from haircuts for the birds to use in building their nests) work together to keep the central tension of the book moving. When Sarah says the dried flowers will give them flowers all winter long, Caleb tells Anna: "Sarah said 'next winter.' That means she will stay." (One of the flowers is even called a "bride's bonnet.") When they throw the haircut leavings to the birds and Sarah says that they can look for nests of curls later, Caleb tells Anna: "Sarah said 'later.'" This must mean that she will stay. When Papa hears about the sand dunes that Sarah loved in Maine, he makes a dune out of hay for everyone to slide down. Later, when Sarah says, "Sliding down our dune of hay is almost as fine as sliding down the sand dunes into the sea," Caleb smiles at Anna across the table and mouths the words "our dune." All of these minor events maintain the central tension by showing us how much the children and the father hope that Sarah will stay.

To make a story believable there must be several levels of development. Too simple a story line—surface-level writing, formula writing—will eventually fail to hold our interest. By contrast, in a story like *Tuck Everlasting*, several story lines operate simultaneously. Throughout the book, they touch at several points. In the prologue, we see what is happening to Winnie, to the Tucks, and to the man in the yellow suit. Later we see the various attitudes of the Tuck family toward living forever. Jesse wants Winnie to wait until she is 17 and then drink the water so they can marry and live forever. He says that Ma and Pa and his brother don't know how to enjoy life. But Tuck wants Winnie to understand that living forever is not what people were meant to do—we're supposed to get on the wheel of life when it's our turn and then get off at the appropriate time. The man in the yellow suit has an entirely different, exploitative view. He will sell the water, force Winnie to drink it, and put her on display—while living forever himself. In addition, there is the toad—

constantly in danger—hopping in and out of Winnie's life. As children discuss the multiplicity of incidents and parallel plots and tensions, they will grow in their appreciation of what makes a really exciting story.

Character

Characters are all-important to story. First, characters live in their own universes: Sarah's remembered Maine coast as contrasted with the treeless prairie; Tien Pao's war-torn China; the sleepy town of Treegap at the turn of the century. In story worlds, characters cope with problems and circumstances that are authentically human. Seeing characters cope, through these literary experiences, clears the way for readers to experience something of what it means to be human even if the literary worlds seem far removed from their own everyday lives. Readers can experience the clearly drawn worlds of good and evil in *A Wrinkle in Time,* can see life through the eyes of a small girl desperately wishing for a mother in *Sarah, Plain and Tall,* can see, in *Caleb and Kate,* that there is always hope for adults who quarrel fiercely to come together again. Books are passports into other times and places, where we can experience the fate of others as if it were our own. Characters, whether human, animal, or preternatural, are the guides who bring the story world to life and teach us to see the rich potential human beings have for goodness, love, faith, and hope, as well as for fear and evil.

For young readers especially, we prefer stories with a limited number of dynamic characters. The main characters should grow, change, and blossom as they cope with story events. We readers grow to know them fully: who they are, what they are like, what their histories are, and what kinds of people they become. Some become friends who dwell comfortably in our memories, and some will come to haunt us in our sleep. We identify with the protagonists and feel negative toward the antagonists, the characters (or things) that keep the main characters from achieving their goals. Both protagonists and antagonists are often referred to as "round"—meaning they are fully developed and usually dynamic, changing in some way over the course of the book. Most books also contain one or more flat, pasteboard characters who are not fully developed, but without whom the story could not be told. These are often stereotypes: an uncaring stepmother, a fairy godmother, a crotchety housekeeper.

We help children gain insight into how characters function in story by focusing on what the characters believe and value. If a question arises, they can return to the text to confirm ideas, to support statements, and to reread what the characters said or did.

Second-grade teacher Lois Wells illuminates character in a wonderful way. When there is a need to make a plan or solve a problem, Lois gathers the children around her and poses such questions as: "What do you think Dominic (Steig's lovable, romantic mutt) would suggest should happen at our Halloween party?" or "How would Dominic view the name-calling that happened at recess?" Once Dominic's point of view is examined, they consider the point of view of another, less heroic character (such as Templeton, the greedy and conscienceless rat in *Charlotte's Web*). Then Lois moves on to having class members share their own views. In this way the children experience the richness that literary characters can contribute to their lives.

Many opportunities will arise in dialogue sessions and in individual reading conferences when the text is used to examine how an experienced author has coped with the problem of bringing a character to life. The children will make spontaneous observations about their books. "I felt like I was right there with Matt," said one young reader who had just finished Elizabeth George Speare's *Sign of the Beaver*. "It was like being in a movie!" This type of identification provides natural opportunities to highlight how character functions in story.

It is useful to help the children realize that characters are revealed in action that is significant to the story. When Tien Pao (in *The House of Sixty Fathers*) rows the airman across the swollen river, we know that he is brave and that he wants to help earn money for his family. When he helps the wounded airman and protects his pet pig with ferocity, we know that he is not only brave, but also kind and loyal. When he stands for hours and days looking into the faces of refugees, searching for his mother and father, we know that he does not give up easily.

As we examine events that seem significant to the story, we also discover how the characters coped with these events. Through this coping we come to know them.

In *Tuck Everlasting*, when Winnie takes Ma Tuck's place so that she can escape from jail in order to preserve the secret of the water that gives everlasting life, we see that she has finally become the kind of person she has longed to be—a person who does something significant with her life, a person who thinks about what is good for humanity.

When we go to the cemetery with Tuck and discover that Winnie never drank the water—

> For it was there. He had wanted it to be there, but now that he saw it, he was overcome with sadness. He knelt and read the inscription:
>
> In Loving Memory
> Winifred Foster Jackson
> Dear Wife
> Dear Mother
> 1870–1948

—we know just how wise and courageous and good she turned out to be. We, too, feel the sadness and regret, but also say with Pa: "Good girl."

It is helpful for children to realize that quotation marks are used by some authors to give authority to important points and to allow the reader to hear a voice other than that of the narrator. It is what Caleb says that reveals how much he hopes Sarah will stay with them ("She said 'later'"; "She said 'next winter'"; "She said, 'our dune'"), but it is Anna's voice that reports what Caleb says.

It can also be extremely useful to examine how an author makes a character believable by keeping behavior true to that character. In *The House of Sixty Fathers*, Glory-of-the-Republic never departs from her piglike behavior, even though to Tien Pao she is much more friend than pig. And Tien Pao remains a small, frightened, lost, tired, starving 6-year-old for most of the book. It is only when he displays almost superhuman stamina in searching for his parents and then in spotting his mother's face among thousands (from a moving airplane!) that we have some questions about believability—moments of doubt that may surface in dialogue about the book.

It may also be useful for children to examine how pasteboard characters who do not evolve differ from dynamic characters in their contributions to story development. When children begin to chart what they know about each character, what their role in the story seems to be, and whether or not they change over time, they begin to see how authors use all kinds of characters.

Authors bring characters to life in many ways:

- By metaphor, simile, and naming
- By the actions they take and the thoughts they have
- By what they say and what others say to them
- By the reactions others have to them and they have to others
- By narration

We know Winnie by what others say to her:

> At this moment a window at the front of the cottage was flung open and a thin voice—her grandmother's—piped, "Winifred! Don't sit on that dirty grass. You'll stain your boots and stockings."
>
> And another, firmer voice—her mother's—added, "Come in now, Winnie. Right away. You'll get heat stroke out there on a day like this. And your lunch is ready."

We know her by what she says herself:

> "See?" said Winnie to the toad. "That's just what I mean. It's like
> that every minute. If I had a sister or brother, there'd be someone
> else for them to watch. But, as it is, there's only me. I'm tired of
> being looked at all the time. I want to be by myself for a change."

And we know her by her actions, as she takes Ma Tuck's place in jail and pours the water on the toad. We also know her by how others react to her: the Tucks love her, the first real child they've had contact with for years, and Jesse wants her to drink the water when she is 17, and then marry him.

Finally, we see Winnie through her thoughts:

> Winnie saw again the wide world spread before her, shimmer-
> ing with light and possibility. But the possibilities were different
> now. They did not point to what might happen to her but to
> what she herself might keep from happening. For the only
> thing she could think of was the clear and terrible necessity:
> Mae Tuck must never go to the gallows. Whatever happened to
> the man in the yellow suit, Mae Tuck must not be hanged.
> Because if all they had said was true, then Mae, even if she were
> the cruelest of murderers and deserved to be put to death—
> Mae Tuck would not be able to die.

Place

Imaginary places created by authors are some of the best-known places in the world. Our lives would be diminished greatly if those places did not exist. In fact, many of us are more knowledgeable about places in stories than we are about those in which we live. Memories and past pleasures are kindled by the mere mention of Wonderland, Narnia, Abel's Island,

and Treegap. Our minds are populated with story places we have visited. It is hard to imagine not having experienced the barn in *Charlotte's Web,* the mystery and delight of the garden in *The Secret Garden,* or the high mountain meadow where Heidi went to live with her grandfather. Imaginary places as diverse as Bilbo's cozy underground home and Narnia under the spell of the White Witch are as compelling as any in the real world. They make up a heritage we all share.

Place is not of equal importance in all stories. In Tomie dePaola's *Now One Foot, Now the Other,* there is no attempt to anchor the reader in a particular place. But in *Where the Wild Things Are,* place is so important that it even names the book. Place, an intricate part of story's whole, contributes to story illusion. Gaining a degree of insight into place helps readers bring story to life in their imaginations and adds to meaning construction.

Attention might be focused on several aspects of place. It may be appropriate to consider, for example, how place contributes to the mood or feeling of the book, as it does in the opening of *The House of Sixty Fathers:*

> Rain raised the river. Rain beat down on the sampan where it lay in a long row of sampans tied to the riverbank. Rain drummed down on the mats that were shaped in the form of an arched roof over the middle of the sampan. It clattered hard on the four long oars lying on top of the roof of mats.
>
> The rain found the bullethole in the roof of mats. Thick drops of water dripped through the bullethole onto the neck of the family pig, sleeping on the floor of the sampan. The little pig twitched his neck every time a big, cold drop of water hit it, but he went on sleeping.

Rain, a rising river, and a bullethole all contribute to the mood, showing us that there is misery here—all is not well.

In some books, the details of place clearly influence character and action, as in *Sarah, Plain and Tall,* in which Sarah reveals by the gifts she brings the children just how much she values the sea:

"For you, Anna," said Sarah, "a sea stone."

And she gave me the smoothest and whitest stone I had ever seen.

"The sea washes over and over and around the stone, rolling it until it is round and perfect."

"That is very smart, too," said Caleb. He looked up at Sarah. "We do not have the sea here."

Sarah turned and looked out over the plains.

"No," she said. "There is no sea here. But the land rolls a little like the sea."

My father did not see her look, but I did. And I knew that Caleb had seen it, too. Sarah was not smiling. Sarah was already lonely. In a month's time the preacher might come to marry Sarah and Papa. And a month was a long time. Time enough for her to change her mind and leave us.

Later Anna turns the white stone over and over in her hand, wishing everything was as perfect as the stone. She wishes that Papa and Caleb and she were perfect for Sarah. She wishes they had a sea of their own.

It may also be useful to attend to the ways in which the author, in creating place, informs the reader about the period in which the story occurs, as in this passage from *The House of Sixty Fathers*:

It had been a long journey. Tien Pao had lost count of all the days and nights. But all those nights when the horns of the new moon had stood dimly in the sky, Tien Pao and his father and mother had pushed the sampan on and on against the currents of the endless rivers. Day and night. There was no stopping even at night. "We don't stop until we drop," Tien Pao's father had kept saying over and over. "And we won't drop until we are far inside this great land of China. Far from the sea—for where the sea is, there the Japanese invaders are."

It is sometimes helpful to determine if place predicts story movement, as it does in this passage from *Sarah, Plain and Tall*, in which a sudden squall on the prairie moves the children, their father, and Sarah into the barn together:

"Wait!" cried Sarah. "My chickens!"

"No, Sarah!" Papa called after her. But Sarah had already run from the barn into a sheet of rain. My father followed her. The sheep nosed open their stall door and milled around the barn, bleating. Nick crept under my arm, and a lamb, Mattie with the black face, stood close to me, trembling. There was a soft paw on my lap, then a gray body. Seal. And then, as the thunder pounded and the wind rose and there was the terrible crackling of lightning close by, Sarah and Papa stood in the barn doorway, wet to the skin. Papa carried Sarah's chickens. Sarah came with an armful of summer roses.

Later Sarah stands by the window and looks out for a long time and finally touches the children's father on the shoulder and says, "We have squalls in Maine, too . . . Just like this. It will be all right, Jacob." And we know that she will stay.

Sometimes it is helpful to examine where an author gives the reader a detailed picture, vividly portraying a place, as does E. B. White in this famous description of the barn in *Charlotte's Web*:

The barn was very large. It was very old. It smelled of hay and it smelled of manure. It smelled of the perspiration of tired horses and the wonderful sweet breath of patient cows. It often had a sort of peaceful smell—as though nothing bad could happen ever again in the world. It smelled of grain and of harness dressing and of axle grease and of rubber boots and of new rope. And whenever the cat was given a fish-head to eat, the barn would smell of fish. But mostly it smelled of hay, for there was always hay in the great loft up overhead. And there was always hay being pitched down to the cows and the horses and the sheep.

Often an author uses place to show the passing of time, as in the sentence "In Max's room a forest grew . . . and grew . . . and GREW" from *Where the Wild Things Are*. Natalie Babbitt also beautifully illustrates this technique in the epilogue to *Tuck Everlasting*:

"Look," said Tuck. "Look, Mae. Ain't that where the wood used to be? It's gone! Not a stick or a stump left! And her cottage— that's gone, too."

It was very hard to recognize anything, but from the little hill, which had once lain outside the village and was now very much a part of it, they thought they could figure things out. "Yes," said Mae, "that's where it was, I do believe. 'Course it's been so long since we was here, I can't tell for certain."

There was a gas station there now . . .

It can also be revealing to find passages in which details contribute to the believability of story by weaving place into the action, as in this passage from *The House of Sixty Fathers*:

He set the ducklings in the dishpan, replaced the mat in the doorway. He did not see that the stake by which the sampan was tied to the bank was lying on top of the rain-soaked ground. One of the buffaloes had blundered under the rope, had scraped it over his bony back, and had ripped the stake out of the soggy ground. The rope with the stake lay loose on the watery mud. Nothing held the sampan to the bank. Inside the sampan Tien Pao still sat chuckling. He had not seen it.

Discovering how different characters value aspects of place gives clues to their interests, values, and commitments and can provide much to talk about when place is important to a story. Consider the following passage from *Sarah, Plain and Tall*:

"Windmill was my first word," said Caleb. "Papa told me so."

"Mine was flower," I said. "What was yours, Sarah?"

"Dune," said Sarah.

"Dune?" Caleb looked up.

"In Maine," said Sarah, "there are rock cliffs that rise up at the edge of the sea. And there are hills covered with pine and spruce trees, green with needles. But William and I found a sand dune all our own. It was soft and sparkling with bits of mica, and when we were little we would slide down the dune into the water."

Caleb looked out the window.

"We have no dunes here," he said.

The importance of place varies with each story. As you prepare yourself for a specific literature study, you will find it helpful to notice whether place contributes to mood, influences character or action, anchors you in a particular period, contributes to believability, shows the passing of time, or gives you insight into the interests, values, or commitments of the characters.

Point of View

Authors take up a position within the imaginary worlds they create. The point of view—the position they take—sets the rules for how much the narrator can be expected to know about the story characters and the events that carry the story action. Determining if the story is narrated in the first or third person is a helpful distinction that can be made to identify point of view.

All children have had firsthand experiences with telling stories in the first person, and more than likely all but the very young have written narratives that document events in their lives. It is therefore easy for them to understand the limitations a writer agrees to when taking the position of the "I" in a story. It is easy to help children see that the narrator of a first-person story can have knowledge of the experiences of the character telling the story, but cannot enter into thoughts and feelings of other characters in other times and places. Readers will be primarily dependent upon the thoughts, feeling, and inspiration of the narrator for constructing their meaning.

Third graders discussing Doris B. Smith's *A Taste of Blackberries* discovered that they did not know the name of the first-person narrator who tells about his friend Jamie's death from bee stings. They solved the problem of what to call the narrator by referring to him as "the I person" as they talked about the story. Such discussions are perfect for talking about point of view. In discussing why the author of this book might have given such an important character no name, readers may well conclude that she deliberately chose not to name the narrator as a way of heightening the immediacy of the events, and of increasing the reader's identification with the narrator who, after all, was Jamie's best friend.

When telling a story from a third-person point of view, however, the narrator can choose to be all-knowing, all-seeing, all-wise, not limited by time and distance—empowered to know the innermost thoughts and motivations of all the characters. In *Tuck Everlasting*, Natalie Babbitt provides a good example of the all-knowing narrator. In fact, in the prologue she gives us a glimpse of what is going on with all of the main characters—the Tucks, the stranger in the yellow suit, and Winnie Foster. As the story unfolds, we see what has been happening to each one, often with the added benefit of knowing their thoughts.

Sometimes writers using a third-person point of view choose to let us view everything that happens through the eyes/thoughts/feelings of a limited number of characters. In *The House of Sixty Fathers*, all our perceptions of events are filtered through those of Tien Pao. We see as he does, and suffer with him as he loses his family and nearly starves (for lack of more than food) during the Japanese invasion of China in World War II. Dejong is so adept at letting us see from Tien Pao's point of view that sometimes we are taken directly into his mind, as in the passage where he tries to deal with fearsome apparitions caused by his hunger and weakness.

First we have Tien Pao's thoughts as Dejong writes: "It must be hunger. It was only hunger. It was only that he was weak and dizzy from hunger. That's what made the spots. There wasn't really anything else."

Then he weaves in a happening—"Tien Pao shook his head to clear it, but fear clamped his heart"—and returns to Tien Pao's thoughts:

> He wasn't alone. They were still there—things on the path! Spirits? Were these the evil spirits of the mountains he'd often heard about in his village? The old people kept talking about them and their horror. How they hid in caves, oozed out of rocks. Now they were coming for him!

Discovering the subtle ways in which a master author works to let us see point of view is one of the delights of literature.

Authors also might choose to be dispassionate spectators, recording what occurs without comment or interpretation, revealing motivations only through what the characters say and do. This dramatic or objective point of view is most evident in play scripts, but it is used in narrative as well.

Most children find it a big challenge to write from the point of view of the third person the first few times they try to write a story. There are so many possibilities when the speaker has access to all ideas, to everyone's thoughts and feelings, and is unrestricted by time and place. When writers take the risk of writing in the third person, it is a big help to be able to examine with them the territory they are entering by comparing it to first-person writing and by drawing on literature to see how other authors have coped.

Time

The art of storytelling is in part dependent on how the teller controls the passage of time. There is no story, of course, if time does not pass. The story may be ordered chronologically, signaled by the orderly passing of hours, days, weeks, seasons, and centuries. Stories may also start at the midpoint in the life of a character, with flashbacks to earlier times and jumps ahead. The ordering of time can create suspense, as in *Tuck Everlasting*, when Jesse goes to tell Winnie of their plan to get Mae out of jail:

> Jesse squinted at her, and then he said, "Yet—you know, it might work. It might just make the difference. But I don't know as Pa's going to want you taking any risk. I mean, what'll they say to you after, when they find out?"
>
> "I don't know," said Winnie, "but it doesn't matter. Tell your father I want to help. I have to help. If it wasn't for me, there wouldn't have been any trouble in the first place. Tell him I have to."
>
> "Well . . . all right. Can you get out after dark?"
>
> "Yes," said Winnie.
>
> "Then—at midnight, Winnie. I'll be waiting for you right here at midnight."

Story time can also be ordered psychologically. Writers have the power to make time stand still, as Babbitt does later in the book:

> In the hall outside her room, the grandfather's clock ticked deliberately, unimpressed with anyone's impatience, and Winnie found herself rocking to its rhythm—forward, back, forward, back, tick, tock, tick, tock. She tried to read, but it was so quiet that she could not concentrate, and so she was glad when at last it was time for supper. It was something to do, though none of them could manage more than a nibble.

Writers sometimes make moments seem like hours—for instance, as we await the impending event of the rescue. Then again, the passing of days, months, and even decades might be noted by nothing more than a phrase, as it is in Babbitt's epilogue, where she lets us know that 69 years have passed since the Tucks were saved by 11-year-old Winnie. As Pa contemplates Winnie's gravestone, he reads the dates 1870–1948 and says to himself: "Two years. She's been gone two years."

Time creates suspense and moves a character along psychologically. Time links the action happening at various levels of the story to the central story tension. In *Tuck Everlasting*, when the author tells us of the cow trail that meanders along and circumvents Treegap Wood, the pace of the story is slowed and we sense that there is something about the wood that is extraordinary. We sense an impending force that is going to change the course of the story, but we come to this awareness indirectly. The pace of this event intensifies the evolving central tension of the story as readers anticipate events to come.

In helping young readers become aware of how time functions in story, you can take note together of how an author orders the passage of time. It may be useful to find examples of how the author has ordered time both chronologically and psychologically. Young readers can reflect on their own lives to understand something of how Meindent Dejong, in his book *Shadrach*, made time stand almost still for little Davy, who waits for his rabbit:

> And what is a week? Poof—and like that a week is gone by. Poof—there is a good week and poof—there it is gone. But a week doesn't go by, and doesn't go by, when you are waiting for a little black rabbit. Oh, a waiting week is long. It is like eternity.
> "And that is long!" the boy said aloud in the dark barn to the little black rabbit that wasn't there.

One group of children was thrilled to discover how the author told them what had happened to a lost pet wolf cub in one chapter, and in the next showed them what was happening simultaneously to the young girl who had lost her pet. Awareness of how time performs in a story can contribute both to readers' interpretations and to their appreciation of the writer's craft.

Mood

The story element of mood establishes the story's limits and pulls the reader into the text. Mood stimulates our imagination and calls on us to make personal connections. Our own daily living and our literary life are put in touch with each other through mood. Created through the use of words, rhythms, sounds, and images, mood intensifies our perceptions and aligns our hearts and minds with what is happening in the story world. The function of mood is to have readers go beyond what is actually said in the text. In *Tuck Everlasting*, for example, we begin with the heat of August:

> The first week of August hangs at the very top of summer, the top of the live-long year, like the highest seat of a Ferris wheel

when it pauses in its turning . . . [It] is motionless, and hot . . .
These are strange and breathless days, the dog days, when people are led to do things they are sure to be sorry for after.

Throughout the story, Babbitt exercises control over our emotional
responses by the way in which she treats the weather:

The August sun rolled up, hung at mid-heaven for a blinding
hour, and at last wheeled westward before the journey was
done. (Chapter 9)

It was the hottest day yet, so heavy that the slightest exertion
brought on a flood of perspiration, an exhaustion in the joints . . .
The earth . . . was cracked, and hard as rock, a lifeless tan color;
and the road was an aisle of brilliant velvet dust. (Chapter 22)

It was the longest day: mindlessly hot, unspeakably hot, too
hot to move or even think . . . The sun was a ponderous circle
without edges, a roar without a sound, a blazing glare so thor-
ough and remorseless that . . . it seemed an actual presence.
You could not shut it out. (Chapter 23)

We move ahead feeling our way, anticipating what is going to happen.
Tension is built and reduced through the mood of the story. Finally, the
storm at the end serves as a catharsis, which releases the tension and sets
everything right:

The first week of August was long over. And now, though
autumn was still some weeks away, there was a feeling that the
year had begun its downward arc. (Chapter 25)

Such writing intensifies our perceptions and makes it easier for us to enter into an invented world that is not bound by the rules of everyday life.

We are lighthearted and laugh as we read of some of Dominic's adventures. We are frightened as we go into battle against the forces of evil in Tolkien's trilogy. And in Robert Newton Peck's *A Day No Pigs Would Die*, we are moved to tears by the death of Robert's pet pig Pinky and by the loss of his childhood:

> My sweet big clean white Pinky who followed me all over. She was the only thing I ever really owned. The only thing I could point to and say . . . mine. But now there was no Pinky. Just a sopping wet lake of red slush. So I cried.
>
> "Oh, Papa. My heart's broke."
>
> "So is mine," said Papa. "But I'm thankful you're a man."
>
> Papa let me cry it all out. I just sobbed and sobbed with my head up toward the sky and my eyes closed, hoping God would hear it.
>
> "That's what being a man is all about, boy. It's just doing what's got to be done."

Mood concerns our feelings as well of those of the author. We are excited, or terrified, or wondering at particular moments of the book. Mood is also the attitude of the writer toward what she or he is writing about.

To highlight how mood works in story, it may be helpful to first identify where we were moved by the story, and then to take a look at how the author moved us. What was it she or he did to grip us or put tears in our eyes? When children share the parts they found funny, or sad, or uncomfortable, it is likely they are talking about mood. They can return to these points in the text to examine the craft and appreciate what has occurred.

It may also be helpful to examine the images (the sun, the Ferris wheel), the similes ("hard as rock"), the metaphors ("a flood of perspiration," "an aisle of brilliant velvet dust," "a ponderous circle without edges," "a roar without sound"), and the rhythm ("It was the longest day: mindlessly hot, unspeakably hot, too hot to move or even think") the author chooses to create the mood he or she wants.

Mood is often created at the level of minor events, and then functions to deepen our understanding of a character or an incident. For example, in Cynthia Voigt's *Dicey's Song*, the mood created when Dicey, working alone, is sanding the boat and preparing it to sail gives us insight into how this young girl, after all this time of being the one responsible for her younger brothers and sister, needs to have something that is hers alone. She doesn't want Sammy to touch her boat. She loses herself in the sanding and lets her mind become free of worry for that short time. In identifying how mood works in story, it may be helpful to examine what happens outside the main story line—all the minor events which, taken together, contribute to our feelings as we read.

Symbol and Extended Metaphor

Symbols in the world of story function to put the reader in touch with meaning that cannot be stated directly—the extended metaphor of the work. Abstract meanings are made accessible to the mind and heart of the reader through symbols. Symbols exercise an unconscious influence on our interpretations. How else can we account for the importance Hildegarde Swift's *The Little Red Lighthouse and the Great Gray Bridge* has for young children? It is doubtful that young readers consciously interpret the overarching bridge as being symbolic of older brothers and sisters, of trying to stand independent of others. Nonetheless, the feeling is there. Aesthetically ordered experiences make feelings accessible in both knowing and unknowing ways. We can experience the import of a symbol without consciously interpreting its significance. For example, as Dominic continues his contemplation of eternity and life and death, William Steig writes that he fell asleep under the vast dome of quivering stars, and just as he was falling asleep, passing over into the phase of dreams, he felt he understood the secret of life. But in the light of morning, when he woke up, his understanding of the secret had disappeared with the stars. The mystery was still there, inspiring his wonder.

In several of his other books, Steig also uses the "vast dome of quivering stars" as a symbol of wonder and mystery. It is present in *Sylvester and the Magic Pebble* when Sylvester contemplates eternity as a rock; it is present in *Gorky Rises* when Gorky floats in the night sky, unable to get down, wondering whether God knows of his predicament; and it is present in *Amos and Boris* as "lying on the deck of his boat gazing at the immense, starry sky, the tiny mouse Amos, a little speck of a living thing in the vast living universe, felt thoroughly akin to it all."

In *Dicey's Song*, when Dicey launches her little boat (after she has finally let Sammy help her work on it), the author lets us know that Dicey herself is also being launched.

In standing for feelings, forces, or concepts present in a story, symbols function to synthesize feelings and contribute to developing story tension and resolution. Symbols can influence story characters and actions, as well as intensify mood. In *Sarah, Plain and Tall*, the same road that winds its way across the prairie and that carried Anna and Caleb's mother away to her grave also brings Sarah to them. In *Sylvester and the Magic Pebble*, we see that Sylvester has gone through the seasons of despair—through the dying of the leaves in autumn and the dark of winter's cold to spring, a symbol of rebirth and new beginnings. We expect, perhaps without awareness of the seasons used as symbol, that spring will bring hope and that Sylvester will be reunited with his family. And when his father finds the magic pebble and puts it on the rock-that-is-Sylvester, and his mother says, "Oh, how I wish he were here with us on this lovely May day," and Sylvester then says, "I wish I were myself again, I wish I were my real self again," we find that "in less than an instant" he is!

In exploring how it was that the children discovered the neglected plants in *The Secret Garden* were "still wick" (still alive), one discussion group decided that the garden (setting as symbol) also stood for Colin and Mary and even Colin's father—all neglected and grayed and hardened persons on the outside, all still "wick" within.

When we ask what a story is about, we are really thinking about story as extended metaphor.

"What is this story really about?" asks the teacher, holding up *Sylvester and the Magic Pebble*. "About a little donkey who collects pebbles and who finds one that turns him into a rock," answer the children. "But what is it really about?" says the teacher, and they begin to talk at another level, suddenly moving to thinking about essence: when you are isolated from those you love and who love you, material gain (what Sylvester wished for when he first found the pebble) fades into insignificance. When the family is reunited at the end of the book, Sylvester's father puts the magic pebble in an iron safe. "Some day they might want to use it," writes Steig, "but really, for now, what more could they wish for? They all had all that they wanted."

In Katherine Paterson's *Bridge to Terabithia*, when Jess builds a bridge for the little sister he previously always excluded, we know that knowing Leslie has changed him, and the essence of the book that speaks to us is that love—even love that is lost through death—need not end. It can be rechanneled.

Babbitt's use of the wheel symbol throughout *Tuck Everlasting* points to the central metaphor as the cycle of life, as Tuck tries to convince Winnie that living forever is not a good thing: the first week of August hanging at the very top of summer like the highest seat of a Ferris wheel (Prologue); the August sun rolling up, hanging at mid-heaven for a blinding hour and at last wheeling westward (Chapter 9); Mae's strong arms swinging the shotgun around her head, like a wheel (Chapter 19); the sun a ponderous circle (Chapter 23); the hands of the clock; the year beginning its downward arc, "the wheel turning again, slowly now, but soon to go faster, turning once more in its changeless sweep of change" (Chapter 25). As they drift on the lake, Tuck talks to Winnie about how the water gets sucked up right out of the ocean and carried back in clouds, and how then it rains, and the rain falls into the stream and the stream keeps moving on, taking it all back again. Then he says:

> "It's a wheel, Winnie. Everything's a wheel, turning and turning, never stopping. The frogs is part of it, and the bugs, and the fish, and the wood thrush, too. And people. But never the same ones. Always coming in new, always growing and changing, and always moving on. That's the way it's supposed to be. That's the way it is."

As readers, we are at our best when we are up to the challenges a good story poses, and successfully bring a unity to the literary experience. When this happens, the story becomes an extended metaphor. The author's aesthetic weaving of events, images, words, and symbols illuminates for our contemplation the stuff life is made of—our experiences, our concerns, and our commitments. In our reading, we seek out bracing reading encounters that call upon us to construct metaphor that opens us to the world, jars us into living more consciously, and helps us not only to see but also to appreciate the range of human experience.

Writers make literary statements that are not reasoned, but imagined. They abstract some of the components of life and order them aesthetically. Good fiction is extended metaphor. Through words, it acts on us as if it were lived life. It tells us to suspend our reasonableness and believe. When it is good, we do. And it is often here that literature becomes something more than just the story that is being told. It makes us think about things we've experienced or thought about, or about what it means to be a human being groping around in this world. It becomes a symbol of something that exists in everyone's life.

CHAPTER FIVE
Teachers at Work

In this chapter we want to describe how it might be possible to organize yourself for literature studies. We draw heavily on examples from our friends and colleagues to show how their programs have evolved—and evolution is the key concept here. We mean the whole chapter to be an invitation for you to begin to try out, to reflect on, and to revise a literature program for yourself.

Working With the Home

Teachers who teach with story greatly value parent involvement. The ones we know work to help parents understand the importance of reading aloud to their children and of having children share with their parents what they are reading.

First-grade teacher Mary Glover hangs a clipboard by the door so that the children can check out any book in the room on their own. They take the book home to read, or to have it read to them. Her students also have a homework folder, and once a week she requires them to take home a book from the "Homework Box" (a mix of easy-to-read, predictable, and wordless books) to read with their parents.

Mary also involves parents when she undertakes an intensive study of one title. Children take home a resealable plastic freezer bag that contains a copy of the book, some blank sticky notes, a couple of pieces of paper, and a letter to the parents. The letter enlists the parents' help in either reading the book aloud or listening to the child read it at least four times before a target date. Sticky notes are used to mark parts that the

Real Reading

By Stephanie Harvey

I don't remember learning to read. It's as if I always knew how. Reading for me was a bit like breathing—automatic. But even so, I couldn't stand school reading—endless purple ditto sheets, mindless workbook pages and basal readers with staggeringly dull stories about kids who looked exactly alike and parents who never fought. As hour after hour dragged by, I would stare at the clock, tap my pencil, and yearn for the end of the day when at last I could race home and read—just read—not answer a bunch of questions, not fill in a workbook page, but read real books. It was in my bedroom that reading captured me, sadly, not in school.

Fast-forward to *Grand Conversations*. Thanks to Ralph Peterson and Maryann Eeds, kids today go off, read real books, and talk about them in school. When they finish one book, they get another and read it. Ralph and Maryann have a deep understanding of real kids reading real books and talking about them. "Children need time to read in peace, to 'just-read' without worrying about having to do things afterward." And they need time to talk about books. "Real books, grand books will provide grand conversations," they wisely remind us.

I return to *Grand Conversations* again and again. Each time I pick it up, I see something I never noticed before, think a new thought, gain a fresh perspective. I can't read it without a pencil in hand. *Grand Conversations* inspires me to jot down my thinking and have my own grand conversation with the authors. Thanks to Ralph and Maryann, anyone who reads this book is better off. Teachers can help kids experience the transformational nature of reading real books and responding to them. And kids will no longer have to wait for the end of the day to head home and read a real book.

child finds particularly interesting or wants to talk about in the group. The pieces of paper are invitations for the children to draw one or more pictures in response to the book. All these items are to be returned by the time the literature study begins.

Linda Sheppard has other priorities in involving parents in her kindergarten program. She stresses the importance of reading aloud (she will demonstrate how to do it, on request), she gives parents lists of authors to look for at the library, she helps them get a library card, and she suggests ways they can build their child's personal library at home.

Both Mary and Linda invite parents to read aloud to or tell stories to their classes. The response of the children to these story-bearing guests almost guarantees that parents will become supporters of the program—part of a close-knit community of parents, teacher, and children supporting literacy together.

Karen Smith teaches intermediate grades in a bilingual community where literacy is highly valued by parents. Often when she sends books home to be read for literature study, parents read and respond to the books as well. She tries to empower her students and their parents. She tries to get the families she works with to see themselves as part of what Frank Smith calls the "literacy club." When one parent expressed a desire to know more about her philosophy, she gave her Ken Goodman's *What's Whole in Whole Language?* to read. The parent brought it back saying, "I had to read it twice, but now that I've read it, I know that's all right."

Karen enlists the parents to help make sure that the students have done all their assignments and to help them pace their reading when they are trying to complete a book for a literature study. She has the parents and children sign a contract (see the example on the next page) describing those assignments, thereby assuring that both parents and students know what she expects.

Karen simply takes it for granted that the parents of her students are interested and willing to be involved, and that she can trust them to work with her in every way they can. She reaches out and the community responds.

Literature Study Contract

Name _____ Date _____

During the week of _____, I agree to read the book titled

_____. This book has a total of _____ pages.

I will pace myself according to the schedule below.

MON.	TUES.	WED.	THURS.	FRI.	SAT.	SUN.

I stayed close to my planned schedule.　　　　Yes _____　　No _____

I finished the book on time.　　　　Yes _____　　No _____

I did not finish the book. I am on page _____.

Student's signature　　_____

Teacher's signature　　_____

Parent's signature　　_____

Grand Conversations, Updated Edition © 2007 by Ralph Peterson and Maryann Eeds, Scholastic Teaching Resources

Our advice for working with the home is to make the assumption that parents are your allies, want the best possible education for their children, and will do whatever they can to collaborate with you. Linda tells us that sometimes she fears that she might be overstepping her bounds; yet when she does take the risk, she finds parents open to suggestions and, in some cases, longing for assistance. Our own experiences tell us that parents universally wish for something better for their children than they had themselves. We urge you to collaborate with the parents of your students at every stage of your program, informing them of your beliefs and practices.

Reading Aloud

These are the goals of reading aloud with the total group:

- To make the language of word artists a part of students' lives
- To make students aware of the delight that can be found in literature
- To help students discover and entertain all the genres and styles of writing (such as poetry, nonfiction, fantasy and science fiction, folktales and fairy tales, realistic stories, satire, classics, picture books) they might never discover on their own
- To develop community through building a common literary history
- To provide a forum for the making and sharing of connections inspired by the reading
- To provide an opportunity for you to help build children's awareness of literary elements

We suggest that you pick a time (or times) for reading aloud every day, one that children can count on and look forward to, knowing that you'll allow (almost) nothing to interfere with it. Many teachers have special rituals associated with reading aloud. Some light a candle, some gather children on a rug so they can see the pictures as well as each other's reactions, and some sit in a special story chair.

Take time to examine the look and feel of the book together before you begin reading. Read the author's and illustrator's names and look at the endpapers, the dedication, or the "something about the author" on the bookflap. Notice when a book was published. These things are not lost on children. When they write, they add their own information about the author at the end of the book. Many dedicate their book to a special person. All proudly list themselves as author and illustrator.

The actual reading aloud is handled differently by different teachers. Some don't like the flow of the story to be interrupted. They discourage questions or comments until the reading is completed. Others allow children to make spontaneous comments. Some want to be sure all eyes are upon them so that they know the children are open to entering the story world. Others allow children to draw or write during the reading. We personally do not like to have children engaged in other activities during the read-aloud time. It is a community event, and we believe children should be present even if they are not wholly engaged in the story.

Some teachers read dramatically, take on voices, and act out parts. Others let the language of the story itself carry the message, and keep their reading straightforward. Reading aloud is an art that improves with practice. It is much aided by having previewed the selection before reading it aloud. Those who feel they are lacking in the ability to read aloud in a way that does justice to the literature and captivates young audiences should make a special effort to practice a selection—to actually read it aloud two or three times—before reading it to children. They may also consider taking a course in oral interpretation of literature, or ask colleagues with more experience for advice and assistance.

When Linda Sheppard reads to her kindergarten class, she does it from several places in her room. She has three different chart racks—one for genre, one for topic, one for authors—where she might record the name of the book.

Her daily readings may come from books connected with an ongoing course of study in which the group is engaged. In their study of cycles, for example, they regularly consult *Chicken Soup With Rice* for comments about the monthly cycle of weather. She will also read from carefully chosen books that make up an author or genre study that the group is undertaking. She prefers to have the children sit with her in a circle, but sometimes she reads from her story chair. She usually prefaces the reading with something she knows about the book. They examine the cover, the endpapers, the publishing date, the dedication, and the illustrations. Then she reads the book right through. She discourages comments during this first reading, because they tend to go off in all directions. But when she finishes that first reading, generally at least half of the group will shout, "Read it again!"—so she does. The second reading is a kind of paraphrase, and comments are invited. She may say something like, "What did you think?" but generally there are children already waiting to make comments about connections they have made with their own personal experience or with other books they know. Her book choices are always part of an overall plan, and the read-aloud is designed to help the children make connections. And because the connecting ideas are already in her head as well as in those of her students, unforced dialogue almost always connects to what they are working on. She says she is constantly amazed at how intuitive her 5-year-olds are about story. They improve over time, but they start out already good at it. "Give yourself time to see it—and listen." She says you must start slow and then slow down so you can see it working—so you can have time to listen to the insights your students will bring to this shared experience.

Finally, she reads the book through one more time. This reading, she says, is the most relaxed. They've read once to enter into the world of the story; they've paraphrased to check out the way the story worked; and finally, they've read the complete story one more time, with the added appreciation and insight that has come from shared community knowledge.

YOU IN YOUR CLASSROOM—TALKING ABOUT THE BOOKS

You must explore for yourself to find the books that are wonderful for reading aloud. There are many sources you can tap for suggestions. Don't neglect the power of picture storybooks as read-aloud material for the upper grades. Although the picture book format may look primary, many of the stories and concepts presented are just right for intermediate and high school (and even adult) audiences. Chances are that if you love the book, your audience will too. Try to read several times a day, from all kinds of text—poetry, nonfiction, chapter books, and picture books.

We suggest that, after reading aloud from your chosen text, you set aside a few minutes to allow comments from your students. Simply ask, "What did you think?" or "What did you notice?" or "What's this book about?" and then listen to your students' responses. Your goal in this simple time of sharing is not necessarily to focus on literary elements or insights, or to critique, but to share the connections your students have made. Be attuned to the way students connect their reading with their own personal experiences. Check to see if they are making connections with other books they have read, or perhaps with those you have read to them. The children will soon begin to relate their accumulating common history to other books they read on their own. They will begin to develop a sense of intertextuality, noticing how so many common themes and events intertwine in story. One kindergartner said when discussing "The Gingerbread Boy," "It's a sly fox, you know, like in 'The Bun'!"

Since story elements (character, place, tension, mood, incident, time, language, symbol, theme) are central to all literary dialogue or discussion or sharing, you may expect these to surface as children talk about a book. We prefer students to discover them in the folds of the literary experience, but it is appropriate to sharpen the focus on them if the opportunity occurs and if the context is right. There is power in naming. When a response raises the potential for developing knowledge about literary elements, or for helping children value their interpretive powers, position it for dialogue by saying something like, "Let's think more about that." Then wait and practice listening with empathy. Try to see where each response comes from. Encourage responding to others and building on other responses. Model for the group the kind of responding that shows respect for the other person's experience. Remember the importance of accepting approximation in yourself as well as in your students. Your careful listening and observation should give you much of the information you need to evaluate your students' progress in making connections. We use a Response to Literature Checklist (see pages 90–91) as an aid for focusing our reflections when we periodically evaluate our students' responses to the literature we share.

MAKING CONNECTIONS WITH WILLIAM STEIG

One teacher read aloud the works of William Steig as part of an author study. She had constructed a chart that listed the titles the children had read down one side and the connections they made across the top. The children made comments like, "Hey, Caleb turned back into himself just like Sylvester and Solomon did!" and "There's magic in all those stories!" (referring to *Gorky Rises*, *Caleb and Kate*, *Sylvester and the Magic Pebble*, and *Solomon the Rusty Nail*). They had noticed the magic, the grief of loved ones left behind, the escapes from near death, the changes of the seasons, and the wonderful Steig-like words like *pazoozle* and *hoddydoddy*. But one of the most delightful periods of connection-making arose the day the teacher read *Amos and Boris*. After reading the part where Steig describes how Amos's strength is giving out and he is beginning to wonder what it would be like to drown ("Would it take very long? Would it feel just awful? Would his soul go to heaven? Would there be other mice there?"), the teacher shared an observation: Steig's characters often seem to be in predicaments where they contemplate eternity and ponder fate in the same way Amos did as he floated in the phosphorescent sea.

It took only that bit of a suggestion for the children to begin to remember parts of the other books they had read. They remembered how Caleb watches Kate move through the house, hopeless now about ever being able to reveal his true self: "And what if she did learn who he was? Would it make her happier? Well, she would know that he hadn't deserted her; but would she relish having a dog for a husband? He decided she wouldn't." And they remembered Solomon's questions after the cat has nailed him into the wall: "Must I stay locked in this prison until it rots and caves in and releases me? That could take a hundred years. Would I still be alive then?" he wondered. "Do nails die?" And they relived Sylvester's imagining of the possibilities and his eventual realization that his only chance of becoming himself again was for someone to find the red pebble and to wish that the rock next to it would be a donkey: "Someone would surely find the red pebble—it was so bright and shiny—but what on earth would make them wish that a rock were a donkey?" Sylvester wonders. "The chance was one in a billion at best." And they also remembered the part of the story in *Gorky Rises* when Gorky, who has made a potion that allows him to float high in the sky, discovers he doesn't know how to get back down:

> He hung there a long, long time wondering where he was—exactly what spot on the map he was over. There was nothing around him but the secret, silent night, the sea of blinking stars. Dreamily, he began asking himself questions he could not answer: Did anyone know where he was? Did God, for example, know? Did his parents?

As the children excitedly retold these parts, they began to discover important connections—insights about Steig and how he thinks and works and writes, and insights about life as well, as they contemplated eternity along with his characters.

One of the marvelous things about studying literature with children is that we grow in our knowledge and appreciation of how an author works and of the beauty of a piece of literature.

YOU IN YOUR CLASSROOM—KEEPING RECORDS

It's a good idea to keep a record of all the books, poems, and stories you read aloud—a kind of community history of experience which, when children look at it, can evoke the experience itself. One teacher fits all the titles into a great patchwork quilt on the wall. Another adds a leaf to a book tree. Linda Sheppard lists the titles on chart paper according to topic or genre. These lists are constantly in use as children go back to refer to a specific folktale, or "cat" book, or book from the list of those they have read by a specific author. One teacher writes every title and author on a sentence strip and puts it on the wall. By the end of the year, hundreds of strips cover the walls. He says that children from previous years will often come by to visit and notice what books he has read so far. "Aren't you going to read *Tuck Everlasting* to them?" one boy asked. Then he paused and looked at the teacher. "I remember how you got tears in your eyes when you read that book. You've got to read it to them." Once the community is built, it lasts.

Extensive Reading

Getting literature going at home and reading to the total group to help children take in the joy of the world of story sets the stage for more extensive and intensive reading.

First this warning: beware that you do not pass by the literary experience—the very reason for working with literature—in your rush to help students improve their interpretive powers. We read to enter into and experience imaginatively a world invented of words—a world that exists in our imagination. The potential value of literature will be short-lived if we ask our students to respond to an experience they failed to have! Keep giving the "lived in" literary experience top billing in your literature studies. Extensive reading is not simply a prelude to intensive reading.

Different teachers manage extensive reading—the time when children are making meaning on their own with little help from others—in different ways. Given what most of us have been taught, it's a challenge to let students read during reading time. It may be a challenge for your students too, who may so far have experienced reading time as fill-in-the-blank time, or as time to sit with the teacher to read tiny fragments of a story aloud. But we assure you that all the evidence points to practice as a major component in helping children become better readers. If you believe children learn to write by writing in a supportive environment that includes demonstration and feedback, consider that in the same sort of atmosphere your students will indeed learn to read by reading.

Once the value of extensive reading is established, teachers and children are likely to face three problems in getting started.

CHOOSING BOOKS

First, there is the problem of learning to select books that will hold one's interest. At first glance this may not appear to be a major problem, but trust us, it is. Adults select books on recommendations from friends, by reading another book by an author they have enjoyed previously, by reading critical reviews, and by browsing in bookstores and libraries. Browsing requires the greatest skill. We learn the reading tastes of our friends over time and seldom misjudge whether the book we are told about is one we will enjoy. But browsing requires that we learn to size a book up on the spot—out of shelves of possibilities.

We suggest that for your classroom library you select books you know already, either from personal experience or by reading reviews. It might be helpful to develop a list of recommendations by keeping annotated bibliographies either on a computer or in a file box and asking children to record a one- or two-word rating after they finish a book. Displaying books with the covers out helps students consider titles. Some bookracks are suitable for this, or you may want to consider installing a simple piece of wood molding around the walls of your room to create ledges wide enough for propping up books. Booktalks by teachers and librarians and by other children are also extremely effective in getting children to consider books they might not ordinarily pick up, as are attractive booklists in pamphlet or bookmark form. We suggest that children consciously try out their skill at choosing, monitoring, and evaluating their success at picking books they really like. The cover may not be the best clue to whether a book is going to be right for them—perhaps reading the first chapter is a better way to choose. Children must work at making choices of books that they will enjoy, and need to become aware of the resources that you, as a sophisticated reader, use to make your choices. Learning to choose books that will hold one's interest is every bit as important as learning to choose one's own topics for writing.

KEEPING TRACK

Next, children need to learn to keep very simple records of their reading on a daily basis. Many teachers use a form that includes date, author, title, and pages read. Some teachers ask that a comment be made about what has been read that day—others do not. Asking students to respond makes sense if the record is serving a function other than simply checking up on whether or not the child is reading.

By allowing children time to read in peace, you model flexibility and trust. There is no need to set arbitrary goals for numbers of books to be read. What is important is the quality of the reading experience. Some children will read Richard Kennedy's *Amy's Eyes* with its hundreds of pages, and others will read several shorter books during the same period of time. It's also important to keep in mind that a good book slows readers down, just as surely as speed bumps slow down drivers. A good story slows us down and gets us to think and feel—and isn't that the reason for reading?

Years ago Charlotte Huck reported a study by Susan Hepler showing that children in traditional programs read an average of two basal readers per year, while children in literature-based reading programs read an average of some 45 books throughout the year (some read as many as 122). Our experience points to even greater numbers. Your students' records give you a way to inform administrators and parents of the success of your extensive reading program.

SHARING

Third, children need to learn to share what they are reading, in pairs and in groups of four or so. This is very important, even for the very young whose meaning-making is fed more by pictures than print. We suggest that you first model how to share books. Gather the children in a circle. Have one child tell the name of the book, and then share whatever it is she or he wants to say with a partner. The partner asks questions and book talk occurs. Next the partner shares, and then the observers tell what they saw and make recommendations.

Once students can work effectively in pairs, practice sharing in groups of four. Practicing under your guidance and taking time to evaluate how the group is doing will ensure success. Children are not only hearing about books that they may not have read yet, but are also learning to cooperate and to hear another child's meaning. They are learning to speak in a group. When they are the only ones who have read the particular book being shared, they are the authorities. They are learning that others want to hear what they have to say. During this time, the teacher should emphasize that the text is not the only thing that is important—that the readers' task is to build meaning out of their present and past experiences, to bring meaning to the text, to project meaning. Willingness to share and to interpret is valued. Children usually share key details important to the plot of the text, as well as their thoughts and feelings, the things they find important.

This is illustrated by the following transcript of a sharing session for Miriam Cohen's *Jim's Dog Muffins*, in which a 6-year-old talks about her feelings of empathy for Jim when he didn't want to talk to anybody because his dog Muffins was run over by a garbage truck.

"I think that's why Jim pushed Annamaria off the bench. Because he just wanted everyone to leave him alone because he was so sad.

"When my cat died I got real sad. My mom cried. That's what happened to Jim's.

"She had a bad infection on her hand and she was having a bad . . . she was feeling sick. And one day we found her in the garage just laying there and Dad knew already. Dad said she was going to die and she did. And so my mom cried and we got long bamboo and made a cross and then after it was all done and it was finished and ruined I put a rose there. I wasn't in school because I was only four when it happened. But if I was in school I would go, 'Let me alone!' and they would say, 'Why are you sad? Why are you sad?' and I'd say, 'Get off my case!' Because I'm sad about my cat.

"When I went to sleep I cried all night until I fell asleep. I cried all night. And then I got up and I put my clothes on all sloppy and I just sat around because I was so sad."

Both Jennie and her sharing group had tears in their eyes as she told about Jim and his dog and about her cat—a moment of clear identification with the character and with the reader as well.

In the following transcript, a fifth-grade boy who was reading Betsy Byars's *After the Goat Man* shares his reactions to Harold's guilty feelings about Figgy's bike accident. (Harold wanted badly for his friend Ada to say that it wasn't his fault that Figgy broke his leg.)

TOM: I felt like that one time, because my brother—he was allergic to strawberries and chocolate and stuff like that and I fed him Froot Loops and he ended up in the hospital.

JOYCE: What happened?

TOM: Well, my brother's allergic to strawberries—strawberries and chocolate. My little brother, he's allergic to like tall grass, dust, mold, chocolate, strawberries—

JOYCE: [*Impatient*] Okay.

TOM: Well, I fed him Froot Loops and the next thing I knew he ended up in the hospital.

BOBBY: You knew that it had something in it that he was allergic to, so yeah—

TOM: Yeah, that's why we had to move out here [to Arizona] because if he had went into the hospital one more time . . .

In this case Tom shares a personal experience, evoked by his reading of the book, which helps him and other members of his group clarify meaning by making connections with familiar events.

The importance for both extensive and intensive reading of establishing these three behaviors—selecting books, keeping reading records, and sharing in pairs and groups of four—cannot be overstated. Without personal responses, without connection to story, we have nothing to build on. A cooperative environment in which children can independently find a book to read, read quietly, keep records of their daily reading, and carry on with quiet partner-talk is a must.

Intensive Reading

When children read extensively, we invite them to extend themselves into the world of literature. The emphasis is upon the lived experience: connecting in personal ways with the story world and actually living in the author's invented world. In intensive reading, the emphasis is on mindful, deliberate interpretation. Attention is focused on the act of constructing meaning.

When extensive reading is firmly established, meaning that (almost) all the children are able to work with a high degree of independence, it is time to consider organizing for small-group literature studies.

Our examples focus on chapter books and children who are reading on their own, but it is also possible for children who cannot yet read certain books to take part in literature studies with them anyway. Many teachers find it helpful to send the book home (usually on a Monday) in a resealable plastic bag or other safe container, accompanied by a pad of sticky notes so children can mark the places they want to talk about. We ask parents to read the book (more than once if possible) with the children, sharing their thoughts, feelings, and personal connections. While the other children are engaged in extensive reading, which for emerging readers involves becoming more familiar with books, reading pictures, and attempting to read the print, the literature study group gathers to talk about their book. Teacher and students share their impressions and interpretations. The time spent actually talking about a book may be only one or two days, depending on the book and the group. The teacher may also want to set aside a time for having the children choose a way to remember the book, through painting, movement, drama, or some other response.

Our own experiences and those of our colleagues have left us no doubt as to the ability of very young children to talk about books with great insight. Because literature is another way of knowing the world, and because story is ingrained in every child from birth, literature studies are a natural extension of what they already know.

FORMING AND RE-FORMING GROUPS

For students who are reading on their own, we suggest the following procedures. Begin with volunteers or select five to seven students to join you in a demonstration literature study. Make certain that the group contains a range of reading abilities. It is important to communicate this value: the study of literature is not limited to the best readers. Literature belongs to everyone.

Of course you are going to have a problem when one member of the group has difficulty getting the meaning off the page, but the problem is an easy one to solve. The child simply needs help. Arrange for classmates to lend a hand, and try to enlist people at home to make time to help the child read the text. Or arrange to tape the story—or have it taped—for the child to listen to and read along. It has been our experience that children who have difficulty with a text frequently have a good deal to offer in a literature dialogue when the book is one in which they are truly interested.

We find it difficult in the beginning of the year to carry out a literature study with more than one group per week. The work is exhausting and intense, and preparation time is extensive. Many of the teachers we work with have sign-ups for literature study, so that membership in groups changes constantly. Most of the teachers we know start in a very structured way. Sometimes they even assign books and group members. But as they and the children grow more comfortable and familiar with intensive reading and with dialoguing together, their students begin to organize themselves. Students show the teacher a book they'd like to study and behave as members of a literacy club, readers who through their intensive reading have learned that delving into the multiple levels of a book can be a joy in its own right.

SELECTING BOOKS

Once the group is formed, they need to select a book for study. Choose two or three books that you know hold good potential for a study and let students make the final decision. Multiple copies (five to seven) of different titles must be available to you. Some teachers ask their librarian to order literature study titles in multiple copies, and they then rotate these through the classes. Other teachers collect the multiple copies on their own, either through book clubs or through a paperback supplier. Check in your town to see if there is a library supply house willing to sell to teachers at a discount. In our area, teachers are able to get a discount of 25 to 35 percent on their paperback purchases. Many administrators and school boards will support expenditures for real books when teachers explain that these books will take the place of more expensive basal textbooks and consumable workbooks.

ORGANIZING FOR LITERATURE STUDY

We suggest that the literature study be conducted in two phases. During the first week, simply ask the children to read the book as they would any book during extensive reading time. The focus is on thoroughly enjoying the story. Meet with the group and set up a reading plan—a group decision about how long they have to finish the book. Chunk the book in pages or chapters so that the children know how much they have to read each day. More demanding books may require a greater amount of time, but for most books a week should be enough.

First Reading

During the first reading you should meet with the group for about five to seven minutes each day to check on how everyone is progressing, ask about the meaning they are making, and find out whether they are enjoying the story. If the children are confused or having difficulty making meaning, plan for specific action. Sometimes you can pair a child who is having difficulty with someone who is not. If more than one or two children have failed to glean simple meaning from the text, you may want to take over briefly to clarify for them what the plotline is and solve the problems that are blocking their interpretations. The children continue to meet for as long as there is something to say. They share what it is that they are experiencing and enjoying. They raise questions about the text and ask for help as needed.

A note on group arrangements: some find a round table conducive to the kind of conversations we are looking for, but some of the best dialogues we have seen took place on the floor. One teacher has a "literature-study rug"—a carpet remnant which is ritualistically rolled out before the study begins. She says that being low on the floor makes her less likely to be distracted by what other students in the room are doing and also seems to reinforce the specialness of this time—a time when no other students are allowed to interrupt.

Critical Interpretation

After the children have read the book the first time, it is time to move on to phase two: critical interpretation. To begin, ask the children what they think, and allow them to share their personal responses and what it is that they liked. While in this phase, the focus will shift to sharing interpretations and broadening the base for comprehension, but it is a mistake to move to this phase too quickly. The teacher's ultimate intent is to get into the text—to puzzle over what the author has written and to encourage children to share what was revealed to them. We work to help children read between and behind the lines, to "fill in the blanks," and to catch glimpses of how the author managed to create the story.

But it bears repeating here that personal response should not be devalued by shifting to a more public attention to print. Readers must never be denied their personal aesthetic experience. All of us project our experiences onto a text—that is how we construct meaning. Our memories, our hopes, our beliefs, and our attitudes shape the meaning we make. Conversely, our experiences are confirmed, or we find ourselves prodded into taking up new perspectives, seeing life in a new way.

The invented world of story works in subtle ways to change us, to reshape our thoughts. Literature is a way of knowing, and in the safety of our reading place, we can test our perceptions in the imaginary world—we can experience a character's fate as our own and use insights we have gained to construct a more accurate view of the world and how it works. Personal response is not only valued, it should be the base for all extended meaning.

The teaching problem is to help children see that responding personally is not all there is to a literature experience. So, once the sharing of feelings and thoughts begins slowing down, it is time to raise the question "What is this book about?" The tone of the sharing shifts at this point, because to respond to this question the children need to analyze, interpret, and seek out evidence for their positions.

It has been our experience that even our adult students are shocked by what they experience in a group that is attending critically to a text. In reading Mary Hays Weik's *The Jazz Man*, for example, several students at first refused to consider the possibility that Zeke, the small abandoned boy who so loved the jazz man's music, may have died at the end of the story. Discussing this book almost always illustrates in a marvelous way what we mean by reading between and behind the lines.

The ability to respond to a text in this way does not grow immediately, so you need to be patient. There is much to learn. When the children are inexperienced in small-group literature study, do not expect them to take the lead. In the early going, you may find that you are contributing more than you would like. Your ultimate goal is to hear more of their insights and less of yourself. However, dialogue is built not only on trust, but also on many concepts that must be acquired. The language will have to be worked on and the concepts demonstrated.

Help children to be intrigued by what the text says and does. After they have read the book once and are prepared to interpret the text from a critical perspective, ask them to use sticky notes to mark the places they want to talk about, parts of the book they found puzzling and intriguing, or places in the story where they had trouble making meaning. We urge our students to mark especially those parts of the story that were so good they had to slow down their reading, or read some spots again, or put the book down for a time to contemplate what had happened.

At our first meeting, we might ask students to share places they have marked, while we try to be ready to pull into focus an idea that has potential for dialogue. During each dialogue meeting, ideas for follow-up will surface, places we want to examine again more fully before the next meeting.

In a study of *Tuck Everlasting*, for example, a session ended with pairs of students taking responsibility for studying those parts of the story that dealt with the toad. They were to speculate on their significance and look at how the author brought them into the story. Another session ended with an assignment to read again about the man in the yellow suit and see how the author worked to give him "such an evil feeling." In another assignment, students looked to see how the author controlled time in the story. Such preparation can function to advance dialogue, provided it is truly anchored in the group's thinking.

THE TEACHER'S ROLE IN THE LITERATURE STUDY

As you meet with your students, let them know that it is their ideas and not yours that will make the dialogue work. Let your expertise trickle out as needed, but avoid domination. Your goal is to evoke, not direct—to focus attention on ideas that are laden with meaning. You act as guide, naming elements in the context of the conversation as they arise and "shooting arrows" of literary insight at appropriate moments for the children's consideration. You can expect that the elements of literature will emerge as the children talk about a book with you. The trick is to recognize and label the elements at the appropriate moment, so that the insight deepens everyone's understanding of the work.

We find that focusing on the elements of literature, thinking in a structural way about what is happening, heightens our perceptive powers. Having them in mind lets us listen for opportunities to call on students to slow down for a moment and reflect on what they are saying. The power of dialogue as a means of constructing meaning is most obvious when you call upon the group to reflect—perhaps with a simple, "Let's think more about that"—so the idea can be examined more fully and its value judged. The teaching challenge is to pick the right moment for the students to refine or extend their knowing.

If we were unable to draw upon elements of story to anchor our thinking, a dialogue would be no more than a collection of fleeting moments. Story elements, however, allow us to position ideas within the immediacy of the dialogue. Through them, we support students' reflections on what they are experiencing or thinking about at the moment, whether they are making connections within the text or gaining insight connecting to other stories in the process of constructing meaning.

You will find that children often dwell on a particular element—discussing character, for example, or incident, or metaphor. It is sometimes very helpful to ask two or three students, or the whole group, to reconsider parts of the book in light of what has been discussed. Children reading *The Secret Garden*, for example, had the following discussion, which led them to consider how character change can point to something deeper. Their discussion reflects the idea that in intensive reading, time is spent contemplating meaning and digesting it. The chief characteristic of intensive reading is this in-dwelling aspect, whereas the chief characteristic of intensive sharing is the heart-to-heartedness of the remarks that each participant contributes. In this excerpt, both the in-dwelling aspect—the thought given to the remarks—and their sincerity (as well as humor) is evident. These fifth-grade children (Shawna and Randy) and their teacher (Mark Routhier) are working through their understanding of the author's message to them.

TEACHER: Since we're talking about Mary and changing, let's talk about Mary and the garden.

RANDY: It started to grow.

TEACHER: The garden did?

RANDY: Yeah. It was like magic. It just started to blossom and stuff. The way she took care of it and stuff.

SHAWNA: I like the way they described how it wasn't dead but it was wickering or something.

RANDY: I think . . . I think . . .

SHAWNA: When you break them in half they weren't dead. They were all dried out, but there were still some roots getting ready to grow—wickered or something like that.

RANDY: Wickered! I think wickered means still alive.

SHAWNA: On the outside it was all dried out but when you break them in half it's still good and they grow as soon as the right time and season comes.

RANDY: Like it's green! Like when you pick a fruit it looks ripe on the outside and you end up biting it and on the inside it's all green.

SHAWNA: Nasty!

TEACHER: Except this is the other way around, though, because she's saying it looks bad on the outside but it's good on the inside.

RANDY: Yeah. Yeah.

TEACHER: I'm thinking about people when you say that.

SHAWNA: [*Looking askance*] You break people in half? [*Both children laugh.*]

RANDY: No, like if they're still alive and they look dead, they'd bury 'em and they'd end up buried alive or something.

TEACHER: Hmmm.

SHAWNA: You see that on a lot of soap operas.

RANDY: Only now they have different things to tell to see your heartbeat, and if it goes then you're dead.

TEACHER: I'm thinking, as you say that, about the characters in the book.

SHAWNA: [*A pause—then a look of dawning*] It seems like Martha, I mean Mary . . . She was like real mean and nasty on the outside, but then later on in the story she taught Colin how to walk.

RANDY: And her outside . . . her inside came to the outside. Like she was mean on the outside but inside she was nice. And then after a while her inside came out.

SHAWNA: All of the good came out. That's when she taught Colin to walk and started taking care of the plants.

TEACHER: [*Writing on a chart that lists insights about character*] I want to hold on to this . . . Were there other characters you noticed changing?

Here the children and teacher discuss character development, but it is only a step more to move to another level as well. They can easily move to talking about what is perhaps the central metaphor of the book—the idea that unlovely people can also bloom when the goodness that is still "wick" within them is nurtured by love and care. Notice how the teacher quietly "shot an arrow" of literary awareness as he brought up the changes in the characters in the meaningful context of the dialogue. He had to do it twice before the children made the connections he was hoping for. The teacher's efforts might just as easily have passed unnoticed. His intent was to offer, without dominating, a possibility within the immediacy of the dialogue.

This teacher had the ability to monitor the dialogue, so that when there was an opportunity, he could drop to the structural level—the level dealing with literary elements that are always present—and help children make connections and see relationships they may have missed on their own. This is a key idea. Not much happens when we stick to discussing particular events within a particular story. If teachers can demonstrate the underlying structure—if they can help children make connections to the elements that make up all of story—then profound insights will begin to occur.

TRIBUTE TO THE FIRST EDITION OF
GRAND CONVERSATIONS

Paving the Road to Literary Understanding
By Linda Sheppard

In the folktale *The Magic Fish*, a fisherman goes back to the sea and makes yet another wish request from his greedy wife to a fantastic talking fish. Pushed to the limit, the fish refuses and the fisherman's wife loses all that she has gained. In the discussion that followed a read-aloud of this story, one of my kindergarten students said, "Of course she couldn't get what she wanted. It was the fourth wish, and everybody knows you only get three."

Ralph Peterson and Maryann Eeds helped pave the long road to the place that made such literary understanding possible in my classroom. Along that road Ralph and Maryann showed me how engaged readers could read, how close listeners could listen, and how a group of disparate peers could talk with one another about the big ideas found in books. I learned how scholars of any age struggle through to triumph when they have the chance to read meaningful text and practice literary critique. I count myself as one of these struggling scholars, with Ralph and Maryann as my humane guides.

Grand Conversations has led countless teachers like me to build with their students a community connected and enriched by story. Today's educational leaders are once again acknowledging that students need schools that assist them in becoming critical thinkers and participating citizens in a difficult world. *Grand Conversations* offers both a careful map and an inspiring vision of how literature can always take us, joyfully, toward this goal.

As children become aware of literary concepts, they will bring this knowledge to other works as well, and will perhaps begin to make connections between similar themes expressed in myriad ways. Opportunities for literary teachable moments occur in every literature study group. Our task as aware critics and group leaders is to recognize these moments and seize the opportunity to build upon them—hence our stress on the use of responsive teaching rather than on a set strategy. You must learn to monitor the pulse of the dialogue—not always an easy task, but one of the most rewarding we know. One comfort is that as you teach in this way there will be innumerable opportunities to hone your ability to react with appropriate responses. There is always another day. You may find it helpful to periodically tape-record and listen to your discussions. You will notice growth not only in your students' abilities to make connections, but in your own as well.

EVALUATING RESPONSE TO LITERATURE AND PREPARATION FOR AND PARTICIPATION IN LITERATURE STUDIES

Many teachers find it helpful to create a checklist outlining their expectations for individual students. Karen Smith uses one she designed for both organizing and grading. (See the Daily Literature Study Record on the next page.) Before a discussion group begins, she asks the children if they are prepared for the day's discussion. You may find it helpful to design a form tailored to your own students and their preparation for and participation in literature study.

We recommend that for evaluating students' work, teachers consider using a checklist that focuses on the behaviors they seek to nurture. You might find the Response to Literature Checklist (see pages 90–91) useful in helping you identify items that are appropriate for your students. We urge you to be selective in choosing items and not try to evaluate every child on everything. We have organized the evaluation into four parts: Enjoyment/Involvement, Making Personal Connections, Interpretation/Making Meaning, and Insight Into Story Elements.

1. **Enjoyment/Involvement.** Certainly one of our foremost goals in teaching about literature is to involve children in story and to see that they find enjoyment—that they take in joy through story.

Daily Literature Study Record

Title of book _____

Date _____

Reader's Name	Brought Book	Prepared for Discussion	Participated in Discussion	Comments

Group Assignment _____

2. **Making Personal Connections.** Nothing is more basic in teaching with literature than to connect students to story, involving them not just intellectually but emotionally. We emphasize that "just reading" —living within the story world—is a must before entering into a literature study where the group will share interpretations and collaborate in making meaning.

3. **Interpretation/Making Meaning.** Literature is second to no other area of the curriculum in offering students opportunities to exercise their imaginations, to engage in critical thinking, and to practice through dialogue the transactional character of meaning construction. Construction of meaning requires initiative, intelligence, and imagination. It is critical to help students along in this area, so making judgments about student progress in interpretation and meaning making is important.

4. **Insight Into Story Elements.** To talk about story is in some way to make use of the elements of story, whether or not we are aware we are doing so. Awareness of the elements provides an opportunity to exercise increased control over our thinking. We want to reiterate that undue emphasis need not be given to the elements that make up story. In fact, we believe it is a poor practice to instruct about them outside of an appropriate context. Making reference to them within dialogue is adequate.

We recommend that you evaluate your students by using the checklist perhaps twice during a grading period, choosing items appropriate for each student. We also recommend that you evaluate students at the close of each literature study, using a form similar to the Record of Preparation for and Participation in Literature Study on page 93. Remember that all of these items are suggestions only; they may not suit your needs. Forms should be tailored to your own students and your own program.

Response to Literature Checklist

GOALS	INDICATORS	Often	Occasionally	Rarely
Enjoyment/ Involvement	Is aware of a variety of reading materials and can select those s/he enjoys reading			
	Enjoys looking at pictures in picture storybooks			
	Responds with emotion to text: laughs, cries, smiles			
	Can get "lost" in a book			
	Chooses to read during free time			
	Wants to go on reading when time is up			
	Has books on hand to read			
	Chooses books in different genres			
Making Personal Connections	Seeks meaning in both pictures and the text in picture storybooks			
	Can identify the work of authors that s/he enjoys			
	Sees literature as a way of knowing about the world			
	Draws on personal experiences in constructing meaning			
	Draws on earlier reading experiences in making meaning from a text			
Interpretation/ Making Meaning	Gets beyond "I like" in talking about story			
	Makes comparisons between the works of an individual author and compares the works of different authors			
	Appreciates the value of pictures in picture storybooks and uses them to interpret story meaning			
	Asks questions and seeks the help of others to clarify meaning			
	Makes reasonable predictions about what will happen in a story			
	Can disagree without disrupting the dialogue			
	Can follow information important to getting to the meaning of the story			

Grand Conversations, Updated Edition © 2007 by Ralph Peterson and Maryann Eeds, Scholastic Teaching Resources

GOALS	INDICATORS	Often	Occasionally	Rarely
Interpretation/ Making Meaning (continued)	Attends to multiple levels of meaning			
	Is willing to think about and search out alternative points of view			
	Values other perspectives as a means for increasing interpretative possibilities			
	Turns to text to verify and clarify ideas			
	Can modify interpretations in light of "new evidence"			
	Can detect implied relationships not stated in the text			
	Is secure enough to put forward ideas that aren't fully formed to benefit from others' responses			
	Can make statements about an author's intent drawn from the total work			
Insight Into Story Elements	Is growing in awareness of how elements function in story			
	Can talk meaningfully about characters			
	Can talk meaningfully about setting			
	Can talk meaningfully about mood			
	Can talk meaningfully about incident			
	Can talk meaningfully about structure			
	Can talk meaningfully about symbol			
	Can talk meaningfully about time			
	Can talk meaningfully about tension			
	Draws on elements when interpreting text/constructing meaning with others			
	Uses elements of literature in working to improve upon personal writing			
	Is intrigued by how authors work			
	Makes use of elements in making comparisons			

Items under the participation segment of the form need to be selected with care. Examples of what we find useful are listed on the preceding form, the Response to Literature Checklist. We find that eight items are about all it is possible to attend to. You might choose elements from our form, or write your own items that fit your expectation of the literature study. To complete the form, add those items you think are most appropriate. We suggest using this form at the end of a literature study to evaluate each participant. Some teachers we know use a working form daily to check preparation for and participation in the literature study.

For those who are concerned about the assignment of letter grades for work that we discuss here, we have included a form developed by Karen Smith—Cumulative Evaluation of Literature Study Participation (page 94). She uses her accumulated evaluations of literature study preparation and participation to make an overall judgment, which makes up part of her students' reading/language grade.

Some teachers use a form to help students develop a reading plan, which is part of the preparation for literature studies. The Literature Study Contract on page 64 may be useful for formulating such a plan with your students. This will help them pace themselves so that they are finished reading at the appointed time and ready to discuss the book. Both this form and the Cumulative Evaluation of Literature Study Participation form help teachers involve parents in accountability for their children's literature study. These checklists also help children feel accountable and refresh teachers' memories over time as well.

As you work with literature groups, you will begin to know which of the children still operate from a silent or "received knowledge" mode. Appropriate notes will enable you to record progress in the children's ability to make connections and to show evidence that they are beginning to think about literature in ways that go beyond the level of personal response.

Record of Preparation for and Participation in Literature Study

Name _____ Date _____

Author _____

Title _____

PREPARATION FOR LITERATURE STUDY

Brought book to group: Yes _____ No _____

Contributed to developing a group reading plan: Yes _____ No _____

Worked according to group plan: Yes _____ No _____

Read the book: Yes _____ No _____

Took note of places to share (ones of interest, ones that
    were puzzling, etc.):   Yes _____ No _____

Did nightly assignments as they arose from the day's discussion: Yes _____ No _____

PARTICIPATION IN LITERATURE STUDY

Overall participation in the dialogue: Weak _____ Good _____ Excellent _____

Overall quality of responses: Weak _____ Good _____ Excellent _____

Referred to text to support ideas and to clarify: Weak _____ Good _____ Excellent _____

Listened to others and modified responses
    where appropriate: Weak _____ Good _____ Excellent _____

Cumulative Evaluation of Literature Study Participation

Name _____

Author _____

	Always		Sometimes		Never
	A	B	C	D	E
Participated in discussion:	____	____	____	____	____
Completed reading on time:	____	____	____	____	____
Brought book to group:	____	____	____	____	____
Completed assignment:	____	____	____	____	____

Overall grade: _____

Comments:

Student's signature _____

Teacher's signature _____

Parent's signature _____

But checklists are only handy time-saving tools. What will make your program succeed is (we say it again) to trust in books, trust in children, and trust in yourself. The children will talk, especially if you listen. When they talk, they will grow in their literary insights and in their ability to talk about them, especially if you model this for them in ways that are meaningful and connected. Expect that you will surprise yourself with your knowledge and insight.

Traveling With Dominic

I f we accept that literature is another way of understanding the world
and that it will illuminate our lives, if we accept the value of the interpretations that all children bring to their reading with a heart-to-heartedness that shows we want to understand why they say what they say, if we
trust that making sense of the world is inherent in being human, and if
we walk alongside our students in the collaboration of true dialogue,
then we can expect that remarkable insights about literature will occur.
But the way is not easy, because each person must do the thinking for
himself or herself. It is much easier to let packaged materials and textbooks do the thinking, to abdicate the responsibility for educating minds
and hearts and imaginations. And on this subject, we leave you with the
words the Alligator Witch had for Dominic when he ran into her at a
fork in the road:

> "I hope you don't mind if I tell you this much," she said. "That
> road there on the right goes nowhere. There's not a bit of magic
> up that road, no adventure, no surprise, nothing to discover or
> wonder at. Even the scenery is humdrum. You'd soon grow
> much too introspective. You'd take to daydreaming and tail-
> twiddling, get absent-minded and lazy, forget where you are
> and what you're about, sleep more than one should, and be
> wretchedly bored. Furthermore, after a while, you'd reach a
> dead-end and you'd have to come all that dreary way back to
> right here where we're standing now, only it wouldn't be now,
> it would be some woefully wasted time later.

"Now this road, the one on the left," she said, her heavy eyes glowing, "this road keeps right on going, as far as anyone cares to go, and if you take it, believe me, you'll never find yourself wondering what you might have missed by not taking the other. Up this road, which looks the same at the beginning, but is really ever so different, things will happen that you never could have guessed at—marvelous, unbelievable things. Up this way is where adventure is. I'm pretty sure I know which way you'll go."

References

Children's Books

Babbitt, N. (1975). *Tuck everlasting.* New York: Farrar, Straus, & Giroux.

Burnett, F. H. (1987). *The secret garden.* New York: Bantam.

Byars, B. (1974). *After the goat man.* New York: Viking.

Carroll, L. (1944). *Alice's adventures in Wonderland.* Heritage. (Original work published 1865.)

Cohen, M. (1984). *Jim's dog Muffins.* New York: Greenwillow.

Coles, R. (1995). *The story of Ruby Bridges.* New York: Scholastic.

Dejong, M. (1956). *The house of sixty fathers.* New York: Harper & Row.

Dejong, M. (1953). *Shadrach.* New York: Harper & Row.

dePaola, T. (1981). *Now one foot, now the other.* New York: Putnam.

Hazen, B. (1979) *Tight times.* New York: Viking.

Kennedy, R. (1985) *Amy's eyes.* New York: Harper & Row.

L'Engle, M. (1962). *A wrinkle in time.* New York: Farrar, Straus & Giroux.

Lewis, C. S. (1950). *The lion, the witch and the wardrobe.* New York: Macmillan.

MacLachlan, P. (1985). *Sarah, plain and tall.* New York: Harper & Row.

Paterson, K. (1977). *Bridge to Terabithia.* New York: Thomas Y. Crowell.

Paterson, K. (1978). *The great Gilly Hopkins.* New York: Harper & Row.

Peck, R. N. (1972). *A day no pigs would die.* New York: Knopf.

Prelutsky, J. (1992). *The Headless Horseman rides tonight: More poems to trouble your sleep.* New York: HarperTrophy.

Sendak, M. (1962). *Chicken soup with rice.* New York: The Nutshell Library/ Harper & Row.

Sendak, M. (1963). *Where the wild things are.* New York: Harper & Row.

Sendak, M. (1970). *In the night kitchen.* New York: Harper & Row.

Sendak, M. (1981). *Outside over there.* New York: Harper & Row.

Smith, D. B.(1973). *A taste of blackberries.* New York: Thomas Y. Crowell.

Speare, E. G. (1983). *The sign of the beaver.* New York: Dell.

Spyri, J. (1962). *Heidi.* New York: MacMillan.

Steig, W. (1969). *Sylvester and the magic pebble.* New York: Windmill/Simon & Schuster.

Steig, W. (1971). *Amos and Boris.* New York: Farrar, Straus & Giroux.

Steig, W. (1972). *Dominic.* New York: Farrar, Straus & Giroux.

Steig, W. (1976). *Abel's island.* New York: Farrar, Straus & Giroux.

Steig, W. (1977). *Caleb and Kate.* New York: Farrar, Straus & Giroux.

Steig, W. (1980). *Gorky rises.* New York: Farrar, Straus & Giroux.

Steig, W. (1985). *Solomon the rusty nail.* New York: Farrar, Straus & Giroux.

Swift, H. (1942). *The little red lighthouse and the great gray bridge.* New York: Harcourt.

Tolkien, J. R. R. (1938). *The hobbit.* New York: Houghton Mifflin.

Voigt, C. (1983). *Dicey's song.* New York: Atheneum.

Weik, M. H. (1966). *The jazz man.* New York: Atheneum.

White, E. B. (1952). *Charlotte's web.* New York: Harper.

Professional Books

Giovanni, N. (1984). Ten years old. In Z. Sutherland & M. C. Livingston (Eds.), *Scott, Foresman anthology of children's literature*. Glenview, IL: Scott, Foresman.

Goodman, K. (1986). *What's whole in whole language?* New York: Scholastic.

Heath, S. (1983). *Ways with words: Language, life and work in communities and classrooms*. Cambridge, UK: Cambridge University Press.

Hepler, S. (1982). Patterns of response to literature: A one-year study of a fifth- and sixth-grade classroom. Unpublished doctoral dissertation, Ohio State University.

Huck, C., Hepler, S., Hickman, J., & Kiefer, B. Z. (1997). *Children's literature in the elementary school* (6th ed.). Madison, WI: Brown & Benchmark.

Iser, W. (1974). *The act of reading: A theory of aesthetic response*. Baltimore: Johns Hopkins University Press.

Rosenblatt, L. (1978). *The reader, the text, the poem: The transactional theory of the literary work*. Carbondale, IL: Southern Illinois University Press.

Samway, K. D., & Whang, G. (1995). *Literature study circles in a multicultural classroom*. Portland, ME: Stenhouse.

Smith, F. (1971). *Understanding reading: A psycholinguistic analysis of reading and learning to read*. New York: Holt, Rinehart & Winston.

Taylor, D., & Dorsey-Gaines, C. (1988). *Growing up literate: Learning from inner-city families*. Portsmouth, NH: Heinemann.

Vandergrift, K. (1980). *Child and story: The literary connection*. New York: Neal-Schuman.

Wells, G. (1986). *The meaning makers: Children learning language and using language to learn*. Portsmouth, NH: Heinemann.

Booklists

isted below are some of our favorite books, old and new. But keep in mind that every year thousands of new books for children and young adults are published, and you may find it helpful to turn to publications like *The Horn Book*, *Booklist*, and *School Library Journal* to keep up to date with the best of the best. Also, Katherine Davies Samway and Gail Whang (1995) have many suggestions for multicultural classrooms in their book *Literature Study Circles in a Multicultural Classroom*.

We have divided our lists into picture books and chapter books, but many picture books are suitable for older readers, especially for reading aloud.

Picture Books

Bloom, Suzanne. *A Splendid Friend, Indeed.* Boyds Mills Press, 2005.
   For anyone, young or old, who has ever been annoyed by a loved one. Notice how the details in the illustrations complement the story ending.

Brown, Margaret Wise. *The Runaway Bunny.* Illustrated by Clement Hurd. Harper and Brothers, 1942. (Many other titles.)
   The books of Margaret Wise Brown have been popular with young children since the early 1940s. They would make a great author study.

Burningham, John. *Mr. Gumpy's Outing.* Holt, 1971.
   Absolutely wonderful words, a classic story shape, and a satisfying ending. For the youngest.

Carle, Eric. *The Very Hungry Caterpillar.* Philomel, 1981. (Many other titles.)
Eric Carle is another writer (and illustrator) whose works would make an excellent author study. There are several that follow the "very" pattern—for example, *The Very Clumsy Click Beetle* (Philomel, 1999) and *The Very Lonely Firefly* (Philomel, 1995).

Chin, Chih-Yuan. *Guji Guji.* Kane/Miller, 2004.
There is much to look at and think about in this story of a crocodile who is hatched by a book-reading mother duck.

Choi, Yangsook. *The Name Jar.* Knopf, 2001.
Unhei, just arrived from Korea, is teased about her name.

Cooney, Barbara. *Miss Rumphius.* Viking, 1982.
What better thing to leave behind than beauty added to the world?

Fox, Mem. *Koala Lou*, illustrated by Pamela Lofts, Harcourt Brace, 1989; *Wilfrid Gordon McDonald Partridge*, illustrated by Julie Vivas, Kane Miller, l985.
Lovely words and outcomes, often with a twist.

Giovanni, Nikki. *Rosa.* Illustrated by Bryan Collier. Henry Holt, 2005.
A beautifully illustrated telling of the beginning of the civil disobedience that led to the destruction of the Jim Crow laws.

Henkes, Kevin. *Julius, the Baby of the World*, Greenwillow, 1990; *Lilly's Purple Plastic Purse*, Greenwillow, 1996; *Lilly's Big Day*, Greenwillow, 2006. (Many other titles.)
Lilly is a wonderful character, encountering very real life problems. Her teacher and parents are worried and wise.

Hesse, Karen. *The Cats in Krasinski Square.* Illustrated by Wendy Watson. Scholastic, 2004.

How cats helped in the smuggling of food into the Warsaw ghetto during World War II. A surprising and moving story based on a true incident.

Hurston, Zora Neale, compiler. *The Three Witches.* Adapted by Joyce Carol Thomas and illustrated by Faith Ringgold. HarperCollins, 2006.

A truly scary story that would make a marvelous collective reading. Children love the words: "O-ooo, Whyncher, whyncher!" "Block eye, chip!" "Hail, Counter! Hail, Jack! Hail, Hickory!"

James, Simon. *Little One Step.* Candlewick, 2003.

For the youngest. Little One Step takes a big journey one step at a time.

Kushner, Tony. *Brundibar.* Illustrated by Maurice Sendak. Michael de Capua, 2003.

Multilayered in ideas, words, and art—a picture book for older readers that chillingly addresses tyranny.

Lainez, Rene Colato. *Playing Loteria/El juego de la loteria.* Illustrated by Jill Arena. Rising Moon Books, 2005.

A warm family story of a small boy who visits his grandmother in Mexico and, unsure of his Spanish, gains confidence by helping call out the cards for the *loteria.*

Lehman, Barbara. *The Red Book.* Houghton Mifflin, 2004.

An eloquent and complex wordless picture book that will delight children of all ages. The book looks like the book! (It would pair well with David Wiesner's *The Three Pigs*, Clarion, 2001.)

Lionni, Leo. *Swimmy.* Knopf, 1963. (Many other titles.)

Another classic of children's literature. Lionni would also make a great author study.

McKissack, Patricia C. *Goin' Someplace Special*. Illustrated by Jerry Pinkney. Atheneum, 2001. (See also *The Honest-to-Goodness Truth*. Illustrated by Giselle Potter. Atheneum, 2000.)

Poignant story based on the author's own experiences. Tricia Ann has a difficult trip to her special place because of the Jim Crow laws in Nashville in the 1950s.

Meddaugh, Susan. *The Witch's Walking Stick*. Houghton Mifflin, 2005.

A fairy tale in the Steig tradition with a most satisfying ending. Meddaugh also has many books about Martha, a dog who swallows alphabet soup and can then talk.

Mora, Pat. *Dona Flor: A Tall Tale About a Giant Woman With a Great Big Heart*. Illustrated by Raul Colon. Knopf, 2005.

A charming Southwestern tall tale, peppered with Spanish.

Muth, Jon J. *Zen Shorts*. Scholastic, 2005.

Wonderful possibilities for talk after reading aloud these thought-provoking tales.

Osborne, Mary Pope. *Kate and the Beanstalk*. Illustrated by Giselle Potter. Atheneum, 2000.

A great retelling of the fairy tale, only this time with a strong, smart, female protagonist.

Perez, Amad Irma. *My Diary From Here to There/Mi diario de aqui hasta alla*. Children's Book Press, 2002.

A young girl writes of her fears about leaving Mexico and traveling to Los Angeles, not knowing the language, not knowing what might happen, and leaving loved ones behind.

Raschka, Chris. *Yo! Yes.* Scholastic, 1993.

A great read-aloud with few words but layers of meaning. Children love to take one of the parts and will do so with great expression and enthusiasm.

Recorvits, Helen. *My Name Is Yoon.* Illustrated by Gabi Swiatkowska. Farrar, Straus & Giroux, 2003.

Lovely multilayered story with illustrations that clearly depict Yoon's feelings first of alienation and finally of inclusion.

Ryan, Pam Muñoz. *When Marian Sang: The True Recital of Marian Anderson.* Illustrated by Brian Selznick. Scholastic, 2002.

Beautiful biography of one of the great American singers. Movingly tells of Anderson's 1939 recital on the steps of the Lincoln Memorial after she had been excluded from the Metropolitan Opera.

Rylant, Cynthia. *When I Was Young in the Mountains.* Dutton, 1982. (Many other titles.)

A lovely memoir of growing up in Appalachia. Rylant writes wonderful books for children—both younger and older. She has many titles in print. Her writing is lyrical and evocative, and often very moving.

Sendak, Maurice. *Where the Wild Things Are,* Harper & Row, 1963; *In the Night Kitchen,* Harper & Row, 1970; *Outside Over There,* Harper & Row, 1981; *We Are All in the Dumps With Jack and Guy,* HarperCollins, 1993; *Higglety Pigglety Pop or There Must Be More to Life,* Harper & Row, 1967; *The Nutshell Library,* Harper & Row, 1962. (See also his work with Ruth Krauss.)

In our opinion, Sendak is second only to William Steig for memorable stories and wonderful words and images.

Shannon, David. *No, David.* Blue Sky Press, 1998.

Hilarious read-aloud for younger students. Kids find David deliciously naughty.

Steig, William. From Farrar, Straus & Giroux: *The Amazing Bone*, 1976; *Amos and Boris*, 1971; *Brave Irene*, 1986; *Caleb and Kate*, 1977; *Doctor DeSoto*, 1982; *Gorky Rises*, 1980; *Shrek!* 1990; *Solomon the Rusty Nail*, 1985; *Spinky Sulks*, 1988; *Tiffky Doofky*, 1978; *Yellow and Pink*, 1984. Also *Sylvester and the Magic Pebble*, Windmill, 1979; *The Toy Brother*, HarperCollins, 1996; *Zeke Pippin*, HarperCollins, 1994; *Pete's a Pizza*, Joanna Cotler, 1998; *When Everybody Wore a Hat*, Joanna Cotler, 2003.

As you can tell, William Steig is our favorite writer/illustrator of children's books. They are all quite amazing, multilayered, and full of wonderful language and offer much to talk about. They delight children of any age.

Weatherford, Carole Boston. *Freedom on the Menu: The Greensboro Sit-Ins*. Illustrated by Jerome LaGarrigue. Dial, 2004.

Excellent read-aloud for upper elementary students who are becoming aware of civil rights history.

Willems, Mo. *Don't Let the Pigeon Drive the Bus!* Hyperion, 2003; *The Pigeon Finds a Hot Dog*, Hyperion, 2004.

Hilarious read-alouds for young children. They love to shout "No!" to the pigeon's entreaties.

Winter, Jeanette. *The Librarian of Basra: A True Story from Iraq*. Harcourt, 2005. What happens to books during a terrible war?

Wood, Audrey, and Wood, Don. *The Napping House*, Harcourt, 1984; *King Bidgood's in the Bathtub*, Harcourt, 1985. (Many other titles.)

Pictures and words work together seamlessly in these books. Much to talk about.

Woodson, Jacqueline. *Show Way*. Illustrated by Hudson Talbott. Putnam, 2005. (See also *The Other Side*, Putnam, 2001.)

A beautiful book in word and picture. Surprisingly moving history of how quilts might have shown slaves a way to escape. The author brings it home to the present.

Yin. *Coolies*. Illustrated by Chris K. Soentpiet. Philomel, 2001.

Told through the voice of a modern-day grandmother as she shares the family's proud heritage, this history of how Chinese immigrants helped build the transcontinental railroad is informative and moving.

Chapter Books

Avi. *The True Confessions of Charlotte Doyle*. Scholastic, 1990. (Many other titles.)

A fantastic seagoing adventure story set in 1832. Charlotte is much changed by what happens to her on the high seas.

Babbitt, Natalie. *Tuck Everlasting*. Farrar, Straus & Giroux, 1975.

One of our favorites for every aspect of literature study—full of beautiful language and insights.

Buck, Pearl S. *The Big Wave*. HarperCollins, 1973. (Original work published 1947.)

The themes of courage, friendship, and the cycle of life and death are addressed in this small and simple story.

Canales, Viola. *The Tequila Worm*. Wendy Lamb Books, 2005.

A vivid depiction of a close-knit barrio community in McAllen, Texas; what it means to be a *comadre*; and how it feels to leave a loving family and become a scholarship girl at an elite school in Austin.

Clifton, Lucille. *The Lucky Stone*. Delacorte, 1979.

> A short chapter book for younger readers. The shiny black stone has been bringing luck to the one who holds it for over a hundred years—from the days of slavery to the present.

Curtis, Christopher Paul. *The Watsons Go to Birmingham—1963*. Delacorte, 1995.

> This book is practically perfect—funny, moving, important, historic, and deep.

DiCamillo, Kate. *The Tale of Despereaux*. Illustrated by Timothy B. Ering. Candlewick, 2003. (Many other titles.)

> An intrepid mouse outcast, a princess in need of rescue, and the power of love and story.

Erdrich, Louise. *The Birchbark House*, Hyperion, 1999; *The Game of Silence*, HarperCollins, 2005.

> These are beautiful Ojibwa historical novels told from the point of view of Omakayas (Little Frog, whose first step was a hop), who was the only survivor of a smallpox epidemic and was found and saved when she was just a baby. Life on the "Island of the Golden Woodpecker" (Madeline Island in Lake Superior) in the nineteenth century is beautifully portrayed—detailed and real, hard but wonderful.

Farmer, Nancy. *The Ear, the Eye, and the Arm*. Orchard, 1994.

> Marvelous fantasy of good and evil in Zimbabwe, two hundred years in the future.

George, Jean. *My Side of the Mountain*, Dutton, 1959; *Julie of the Wolves*, Harper & Row, 1972.

> Classic survival stories with memorable characters and concern for the natural world.

Hamilton, Virginia. *The Planet of Junior Brown*, Macmillan, 1967; *M.C. Higgins the Great*, Macmillan, 1967; *The House of Dies Drear*, Macmillan, 1968.

Incredible writing, struggle, hope, history, and small acts that change the world.

Hesse, Karen. *Aleutian Sparrow*. Margaret K. McElderry, 2003.

A little-known event during World War II—the moving of the Aleuts from their ancestral home to camps where they were all but decimated—is told in Hesse's signature "story in poetry" style.

Himelblau, Linda. *The Trouble Begins*. Delacorte, 2005.

Du Nguyen is a dragon to his grandmother, but to the family in California he has just joined after years of separation, he is one trouble after the next. This funny and poignant story is full of insights about what it's like to be an immigrant boy with a different culture and language.

Ibbotson, Eva. *Journey to the River Sea*, Dutton, 2002; *The Star of Kazan*, Dutton, 2004.

Both of the books are rollicking adventure stories with strong female protagonists. The first is set in the Amazon in the early twentieth century, the second in Austria and Germany in the same period. Both feature orphaned or abandoned young girls, mysteries, wonderful descriptions of place, and supremely satisfying endings.

Johnson, Jane. *The Secret Country: The Eidolon Chronicles*. Simon & Schuster, 2006.

This book begins with a talking cat who insists 12-year-old Ben take him home. Funny, gripping, good-versus-evil fantasy. A fourth grader told me this was the best book he'd ever read.

Kadohata, Cynthia. *Weedflower*. Atheneum, 2006.

> Based on the author's family history, this is a beautifully written story of Sumiko and her family, forced from their home and flower gardens in coastal California to a relocation camp in the desert of the Colorado River Indian Tribes' reservation during World War II. Friendship, gardens, and art save her and others from despair.

Konigsburg, E. L. *The Outcasts of 19 Schuyler Place*, Atheneum, 2004; *Silent to the Bone*, Atheneum, 2000; *The View From Saturday*, Atheneum, 1996; *From the Mixed-Up Files of Mrs. Basil E. Frankweiler*, Atheneum, 1967; *Jennifer, Hecate, Macbeth, William McKinley and Me, Elizabeth*, Atheneum, 1971.

> Konigsburg is a master at creating funny, brilliant, out-of-the-ordinary characters. Mystery is often a factor in the books, along with important ideas and psychological truths.

LaFaye, A. *Worth*. Simon & Schuster, 2004.

> An exploration of what it might have been like to have been—and to have taken in—one of the Orphan Train children of the late nineteenth century. Contrasts the harsh life of ranching and farming in Nebraska with the equally harsh tenement life of the city.

Le Guin, Ursula K. The Earthsea Cycle, books 1–4: *A Wizard of Earthsea*, Parnassus, 1968; *The Tombs of Atuan*, Atheneum, 1971; *The Farthest Shore*, Atheneum, 1972; *Tehanu*, Atheneum, 1990.

> A beautiful and classic fantasy series for more mature readers. *Tehanu* is an especially wonderful book. Important ideas, masterful writing.

L'Engle, Madeleine. *A Wrinkle in Time*. Farrar, Straus & Giroux, 1962.

> Still a wonderful book—an adventure, a fantasy, and a tribute to the power of love.

Lewis, C. S. *The Lion, the Witch and the Wardrobe*. Macmillan, 1961.
   The first of the Chronicles of Narnia, the still-loved classic fantasy series that can be read on many levels.

Lin, Grace. *The Year of the Dog*. Little, Brown, 2005.
   A lovely book for younger readers especially—full of the author's drawings (great instructions on how to draw a dog) and full of incidents based on the author's life. How Pacy/Grace made it through her special year makes a perfect story. Lin says she wrote it because she never saw herself, a Taiwanese American, in any of the books she read as a child.

Lowry, Lois. *The Giver*. Houghton Mifflin, 1993.
   Science fiction futuristic fantasy where every aspect of life is controlled.

Lowry, Lois. *Number the Stars*. Houghton Mifflin, 1989.
   World War II Holocaust novel that is appropriate for younger readers.

MacLachlan, Patricia. *Sarah, Plain and Tall*. Harper & Row, 1985.
   A tiny chapter book full of possibilities for talk.

Magorian, Michelle. *Good Night, Mr. Tom*. Harper & Row, 1981.
   World War II story of a small abused boy evacuated to an English village and assigned to Mr. Tom.

Mathis, Sharon Bell. *The Hundred Penny Box*. Illustrated by Leo Dillon and Diane Dillon. Viking, 1975.
   This heartwarming story of a small boy who loves his old great-great-aunt, Dew, and looks after the box that holds her life is almost a chapter book for younger readers.

Paterson, Katherine. *The Same Stuff as Stars*. Clarion, 2002. (See also *The Great Gilly Hopkins*, HarperCollins, 1978; *Bridge to Terabithia*, HarperCollins, 1977; and *Lyddie*, Dutton, 1991.)

Angel is almost as memorable a character as the great Gilly Hopkins. Paterson again explores what it takes to make a family.

Paulsen, Gary. *Hatchet*. MacMillan, 1986.

Classic survival/adventure story—dramatic and gripping.

Riordan, Rick. *Percy Jackson and the Olympians: The Lightning Thief—Book One*, Miramax, 2005; *Percy Jackson and the Olympians: The Sea of Monsters—Book Two*, Miramax, 2006.

The Olympian Gods are still alive and operating in the twenty-first century. (Mount Olympus is above the Empire State Building.) Percy is Perseus, half-god, half-boy. A whole new look at ancient myths—funny, gripping, and full of tension.

Rowling, J. K. *Harry Potter and the Sorcerer's Stone* (book 1), Arthur A. Levine, 1998; *Harry Potter and the Chamber of Secrets* (book 2), Arthur A. Levine, 1999; *Harry Potter and the Prisoner of Azkaban* (book 3), Arthur A. Levine, 1999; *Harry Potter and the Goblet of Fire* (book 4), Arthur A. Levine, 2000; *Harry Potter and the Order of the Phoenix* (book 5), Arthur A. Levine, 2003; *Harry Potter and the Half-Blood Prince* (book 6), Arthur A. Levine, 2005.

The Harry Potter books are a worldwide phenomenon. They are full of gripping tension, magic, friendship, humor, and tragedy. The earlier books are suitable for younger readers; the later books are much darker.

Ryan, Pam Muñoz. *Becoming Naomi León*. Scholastic, 2004.

Naomi and Owen have a bad mother who abandoned them years ago and who now wants to take Naomi (but not Owen) away from the life they live in a little trailer with their grandmother. Gram, Naomi, and Owen flee to Mexico, where Naomi discovers and appreciates who she is and who she will be.

Ryan, Pam Muñoz. *Esperanza Rising.* Scholastic, 2000.

> Lovely historical novel based on the life of the author's own grand-mother. Esperanza is a wealthy Mexican girl, very aware of class differences, when sudden misfortune totally changes her and her mother's circumstances and they are forced to come north to the United States. A gripping portrayal of the tension between the groups trying to survive during the days of the dust bowl migration.

Schmidt, Gary. *Straw Into Gold.* Clarion, 2001.

> This book is dark and somewhat violent, but it is a gripping adventure that explains why Rumpelstiltskin wanted that little baby prince in the first place. For mature readers.

Stauffacher, Sue. *Donuthead,* Knopf, 2003; *Harry Sue,* Knopf, 2005.

> *Donuthead* would be a great read-aloud, although it might bring up a lot of questions since the hero, Franklin Delano Donuthead, is the child of a single mother (a capable person) and a sperm donor. He also suffers from obsessive-compulsive disorder. Funny dialogue, great characters, insights into bullying. The main character in *Harry Sue* is almost too much to accept—a child with both parents in prison, one for throwing her out a window, the other for making methamphetamine for sale. (Stauffacher deals with the "now.") But what a wonderful, lovable, memorable character Harry Sue is. As with each of the recommended books, read it first and see what you think.

Steig, William. *The Real Thief,* Farrar, Straus & Giroux, 1973; *Dominic,* Farrar, Straus & Giroux, 1972; *Abel's Island,* Farrar, Straus & Giroux, 1976.

> Three wonderful books. *The Real Thief* is a tiny chapter book, suitable for very young readers. *Dominic* and *Abel's Island* are multilayered classics for all ages and can be read again and again.

Voigt, Cynthia. *Homecoming*, Atheneum, 1981; *Dicey's Song*, Atheneum, 1982. (Many other titles.)

These are wonderfully written, multilayered books about what happens to four abandoned children—part of the Tillerman series.

White, E. B. *Charlotte's Web*. Harper, 1952.

A beautifully written classic.

Yep, Lawrence. *Dragonwings*. Harper & Row, 1977.

On the West Coast, a Chinese immigrant made an airplane about the same time as the Wright Brothers in the east. This is a lovely story of friendship despite differences, perseverance, and survival during the 1906 earthquake.

Tribute Authors

Ardith Davis Cole, author of *Knee to Knee, Eye to Eye: Circling in on Comprehension* and *When Reading Begins: The Teacher's Role in Decoding, Comprehension, and Fluency*

Mary Glover, author of *Surprising Destinations: A Guide to Essential Learning in Early Childhood* and *Two Years: A Teacher's Memoir* and coauthor of *Not on Your Own: The Power of Learning Together*

Stephanie Harvey, coauthor of *Strategies That Work: Teaching Comprehension to Enhance Understanding* and *The Comprehension Toolkit: Language and Lessons for Active Literacy*

Lester Laminack, author of *Cracking Open the Author's Craft* and coauthor of *Learning Under the Influence of Language and Literature*

Frank Serafini, author of *Around the Reading Workshop in 180 Days* and *Lessons in Comprehension*

Linda Sheppard, coauthor of *Not on Your Own: The Power of Learning Together*

Suzette Youngs, coauthor of *Around the Reading Workshop in 180 Days* and *Writing Without Boundaries: What's Possible When Students Combine Genres*